# Praise for Living HIPP

"Pam Guyer still has her groove! From a girl jumping on her bed belting out lyrics, to a woman making her own 'music,' she empowers women to be their best from the inside out. In this wonderfully written book filled with exercises and tips, Pam holds no punches—life can be hard. But we all have in common the right to choose. Take up this book, *Living HIPP*, and find what turns you on to life; you might not make the top 10 on the charts . . . but you will be authentically you."

—***Sallie Felton,*** *Life Coach, Bestselling Author, Inspirational Speaker, and International Radio Talk Show Host*

"Bravo 'HIPP' Pam! What a 'feel-good' experience reading this book is. Every girl (young and well... older) will be uplifted and encouraged that she really is HIPP. Thank you for helping women discover their HIPPness! I'm looking forward to more HIPP books, because like *Chicken Soup for the Soul,* your message is so relevant."

—***Donna Johnson,*** *Executive National Vice President, Arbonne and Founder of Spirit Wings Kids, Inc.*

"Women are busy, and we have big goals. To fulfill our dreams and get more out of life, we have to approach life with the right mindset and a plan of action. *Living HIPP* will help you do both. Dust off your dreams, then decide which actions you need to take to move toward reaching your goals."

— ***Allyson Lewis****, Time Strategist and Author of* The 7 Minute Solution

"Pam Guyer's message of reaching out and helping others stand up for themselves is right on target. It's time to stop worrying about what others think. Do your best and help others do their best. Inspire others to success by paving the way. Live HIPP."

—***Dan Miller****, Creative Thinker at 48Days.net and Author of* 48 Days to the Work You Love

"*Living HIPP* is a must read for any woman who is looking to live her best life. Not only will you learn practical tips on how to dream, set goals, and achieve, you will also learn how to create a HIPP lifestyle and relationships. Pam's mission to create generations of positive, strong, confident women is a worthy one. Get the book, and get HIPP!"

—***Chris Widener****, Bestselling Author of* The Art of Influence *and* The Leadership Rules

# Living HIPP

### Happy. Inspired. Passionate. Peaceful.

## Own your life.

Pam Guyer

*To my husband Charlie Guyer: You are my true companion,*
*best friend, and the best guy ever.*

*To my beautiful babies...*
*Kaili, you are the epitome of HIPP. Every girl should follow*
*your example. You are beautiful.*
*Cameron and Colby, I adore my boys and am so proud of you*
*both for your kind hearts and zest for life.*

*I love my family more than anything.*
*There's no feeling like HIPP, and there's no place like home!*

# Contents

Foreword by Rita Davenport .............................................. ix
Introduction .............................................. 1

## Discover Your HIPP Life

Life Happens .............................................. 15
(Re-) Discover Your Dreams .............................................. 29
Cast a Vision for Your Life .............................................. 47

## Making HIPP Your Reality

Live Happy .............................................. 73
Live Inspired .............................................. 89
Live Passionate .............................................. 101
Live Peaceful .............................................. 113

## Living HIPP: Day In and Day Out

Clean House .............................................. 125
Own Yourself! .............................................. 149
Live Well .............................................. 167
Get HIPP! .............................................. 179
HIPP Generation .............................................. 189

Acknowledgements .............................................. 199
About the Author .............................................. 207

# Foreword

For decades, our culture has been marked by the pursuit of material wealth. The idea was that fancy clothes made the man (or woman); the bigger the house and more exotic the vacations, the better; and goodness knows you need gobs of money to be happy, right? Wrong! Those are all things that we can't take with us. I've never seen a hearse with a U-Haul® behind it; have you?

Thankfully, one of the blessings that resulted from the dip our economy has taken in the past few years is that people have started to come back to their senses about what's really important in their lives. The experiences we have, the character we are known for, and above all, the way we treat and interact with other people are what truly matter.

I've been teaching a "people first" philosophy for years. In my opinion, it's the best and only way to live. When you show people how much you love them and when you help and serve others, success will come to you in ways you could never imagine.

But, before you can really give your all to others, you have to become your best self. You have to "mind your mind" and work on creating a positive attitude that keeps you going when life gets hard. And it is work! Most people don't just wake up every day feeling great. In my work as a former television host and president of an international direct selling company, and today as an author, trainer, encourager, and motivational speaker, I've delivered well over one thousand speeches on how to live more, do more, be more, learn more, and earn more so you can give more. I've talked about how important a positive attitude is—how it shapes our lives, our families, and our success. But don't think for a minute that I wake up every day raring to go. No, sometimes you're tired. Sometimes your children, or your business, or your family members, or your history weighs you down. That's when you have to go deep inside yourself and pull out the real you. The "real" you is the person you want to be, the person you work to be, the person you're sent here to be.

Do you remember when Flight 1549 made an emergency landing on the Hudson River back in 2009? Captain Sullenberger's words to the passengers and crew just before that heroic landing touched me. He said, "Brace for impact." Isn't that what we have to do, too? We've recently seen how job loss and stock market tumbles can rock our world. And you probably know from firsthand experience what it's like to deal with death, disease, or heartbreak. If you aren't braced, or prepared, for the tough times—not just financially, but emotionally, spiritually, mentally as well—they can take you down. That's why you must work, now, on becoming the person you want to be. To become that person, you have to get control of your attitude and mindset. When those two things are in the right place, you are better equipped to share and show love to your family and everyone around you, no matter what circumstances you encounter.

When you are focused on being your best self, you don't worry about arriving at a destination. School is never out for the "pro," and school is never out for the HIPP girl, either. It's the journey that matters most. This book will ignite your desire to grow even more and become even more.

One of the things that thrills me most in this world is seeing people fly past their expectations and into their dream life. I've seen Pam Guyer do that. During the past ten years, it has been my privilege to watch Pam grow her business by loving on people. She walks the talk when it comes to building others up and living "people first." Her heart for helping women and teens stand up for themselves is evident in not only her words, but in the way she lives her life. I believe she's able to be that type of encourager because she worked on preparing herself for impact. She'll tell you in this book about some of the experiences that shaped her life—and how she had to move past old hurts and develop an unwavering belief in herself. She'll also share practical ideas on how to live a happy, inspired, passionate, and peaceful life. And while Pam refers to herself as a cheerleader, the advice she shares isn't just "Rah-Rah-Rah!" It's *real*. Because what she's learned and what I know, is that when you mind your mind, believe in yourself, focus on what you really want, and then *do the work*, you can do, be, and have whatever you want in life.

This HIPP Generation and culture is something I have been teaching for decades, and I know Pam's mission and heart is to help create a movement that inspires people to encourage and empower others. From the moment I met Pam, I knew she was someone who would shake things up; I'm glad God put me on this earth the same time as her! She is talented, gifted, caring —a true treasure. In this book, you'll hear Pam's heart and her desire for you to stand up for yourself and own your life. Get ready; Pam Guyer and her message in *Living HIPP* is about to rock your world. You'll be moved, uplifted, and educated by a talented example of what's really important in life and how to measure success. Your job, then, is to take that message and pass it on.

This book is a must read for any woman who desires to live her best life; it is for you. Not only will it equip you to create your best life, it will teach you the importance of encouraging others. When you put what you learn in *Living HIPP* into action, I believe you can live your dream life, too. Don't wait. Start now. You'll find yourself laughing, crying, and nodding in agreement. Don't let this awesome experience pass you by.

**Rita Davenport**
*Author, Motivational Speaker, Encourager, Trainer*

# INTRODUCTION

**S**ome days you feel *HIPP*: Happy, Inspired, Passionate, and Peaceful. On those days, you've got your groove on. Your kids behave perfectly, your husband remembers to pick up his boxers off the floor, your hair looks amazing, your house stays clean all day, and customers call asking to buy from you.

For most of us those days are few and far between.

And it's not because you don't try. You may even *appear* HIPP to others. You may have the right title, the right clothes, and good friends; but on the inside you feel fragmented, disconnected, and stretched thin—like a one-woman three-ring circus, juggling, spinning plates, and fighting back the lions, all at the same time. No wonder you're exhausted!

And then you see *her*. You know who I mean. She could be a Hollywood celebrity or your next-door neighbor. She has the perfect body, perfect life, perfect family, and perfect job.... She makes you perfectly ill. You look at her and think: *Well, no wonder! If I had an assistant, a nanny, a rich husband, a cook, good genes, and a personal trainer, I could be perfect, too!*

The truth is, nobody's perfect. If you could peek into my life, you'd see that I have my HIPP moments, even a few, fully HIPP days now and then. You'd also see that there are times when my lovable, wonderful, close-to-perfect children drive me absolutely crazy. You'd see how much I adore my husband. You'd also see how he, too, has mastered the art of

---

When you're HIPP, you empower yourself
to become your absolute best,
strongest self, and you
encourage others to do the same.

---

making me insane. You'd see how passionate I am about my business, and at the same time you'd see how challenging it is to balance my work, kids, marriage, health, and sanity. You'd see me devour an entire bag of M&M'S® in a moment of total stress and *un*HIPPness. You'd see that there are days when I look at the seemingly perfect women in my life and think: *Why can't I get my act together like them?*

Here's the good news: You don't have to be perfect to Live HIPP. In fact, I prefer you not be. Being HIPP means allowing your vulnerabilities and weaknesses to fuel the fire within you. Living HIPP is making the most of your strengths *and* your challenges and laughing your way to better living. You know you are Living HIPP when your life is chaotic and messy, and you *choose* to take on the day anyway with a hands-on-hips attitude filled with heart and determination.

# What is HIPP?

HIPP is your beautiful life as *you* define it. It is getting up each morning with an intention to enjoy the day. Living HIPP doesn't mean you're living in Utopia, but that you focus on making daily progress and improvements to yourself and your life. When you're HIPP, you empower yourself to become your absolute best, strongest self, and you encourage others to do the same. When you're Living HIPP, you are casting a vision, following your passion, and making bold steps to live the life you want.

You already know what HIPP stands for, but let's take a few minutes to define the words that comprise HIPP:

## H*appy*

Everyone wants to be happy. Next to good health, happiness is the simple truth we all desire in our life. But what does happy mean? My definition of *happy* is feeling joyful despite the chaos of life and accepting that chaos is not always joyful. When you're truly happy, you can feel peaceful even when challenges arise.

I believe happiness is a natural result of creating the life you desire, as opposed to letting life happen to you. That's what I hope *Living HIPP* will inspire you to do. My goal is to help every girl and woman in the world worry less and be happy *more*. My intention is to help you grab hold of the happiness you deserve, to celebrate you, your life, and the spirit within you. After all, if you have only one life to live, why not make it an intensely happy one?!

## INSPIRED

One definition of the word *inspire* is "to fill with revolutionary ideas." Another is "to encourage or incite action." To live an inspired life you must intentionally and continually fill your mind with words, sights, and sounds that move you to action. Being inspired isn't passive. It isn't simply feeling good because you've heard a moving song or speech. True inspiration fills you with ideas that motivate you to take *action*.

I hope that as you read this book, you will be inspired to let go of the things, people, and behaviors that aren't serving you well. I want you to find the courage to create the life you really want, and that requires action! My intention is that, ultimately, you will be moved to empower other people to live HIPP.

## Passionate

If inspiration is the spark that lights the fire, passion is the white-hot, eternal flame that propels you forward. Your passion is your mission and purpose in life. It's what drives you to put in the time, effort, blood, sweat, and tears necessary to make your dreams come to life. When you live with passion, you become *unstoppable*.

Stop and think about that last statement for a minute. If you are living and pursuing your passion, you should be unstoppable. You should be able to blast through roadblocks, push through energy slumps, and deal with daily challenges without missing a beat. Is that true for you? Or, are you frequently tangled up by worry and time-wasters.

Are you easily distracted by shiny objects or the *ding* of in-coming emails? My guess is that if greener grass constantly grabs your attention, it may be because you haven't iden-tified your true passion. Author-humorist Erma Bombeck said it cleverly: *The grass is always greener over the septic tank.* The lesson here: If you *are* living your passion and things still aren't going your way, don't bolt. It may be that you need to allow yourself to go through all the seasons. It may

---

HIPP is living with purpose.
It is choosing to be happy, inspired,
passionate, and peaceful, today.

---

feel like winter but spring is on the way. It's far better to have fresh, spring showers watering your pasture from above, than septic tank water feeding it from below!

Throughout this book I'm going to ask you to think about what you really want. Your passion comes from inside *you*. It isn't what your mom or dad wants for you, or what your boss wants for you, or what your friends say you should do, or what you get by trying to be like someone else. Your passion is personal; it's unique to you. And when you begin to pursue *your* passion, you'll know you're making the right choices for yourself.

## Peaceful

If you're concerned I'm about to tell you to find a comfortable position on your yoga mat, relax. Being peaceful isn't about sitting still in the Lotus position while chanting, "Om," but later in this book you'll learn why I believe activities like yoga can be incredibly effective.

Modern women are constantly pursuing something. Most of the time we want more: more time, more money, more opportunity, better health, more joy, more abundance, more peace, or more love. Sometimes we want *less:* less clutter, less drama, less anger, less debt, fewer negative people, less dirty laundry (literally and figuratively). We put intense pressure on ourselves to perform, produce, compete, connect, achieve, look good, be fit, lose weight, be there, and stand out. In other words: to *do it all.*

My goal with this book is to teach you not to do it *all.* Being peaceful is about releasing the valve and decreasing the pressure. It is time to simplify, to relax, and to be at peace with who you are and what you have right now.

HIPP is living with purpose. It is choosing to be happy, inspired, passionate, and peaceful, today. Living HIPP means that when you fall down—because you will—you choose to stand up even stronger. It's about laughing at yourself, making light of what you can, and easing up on yourself and others.

## My HIPP Life

Speaking of pressure, do you know how stressful it is to write a book about Living HIPP? When I gave birth to the

HIPP brand, I was on fire! I knew HIPP living would change the world. "Get Oprah on the phone," I told my husband. "This is going to be huge!" After all, what could be better than living a happy, inspired, passionate, peaceful life? But when the HIPP buzz wore off, fear and doubt set in. *How can I write a book on being happy, inspired, passionate, and peaceful when I don't always feel those things? Maybe*, I thought, *I should just write a book about being a HIPPocrite: a harried, incomplete, procrastinating, pissed off, relationship-challenged, irritated, tail-chaser.*

There are plenty of days when I have to *fight* to live HIPP. The pragmatic part of me jeers and says, "Get real! Give up. Give in. What's the point of trying to live HIPP when you're dealing with all this crap?" But deep down, I know that little

---

*Rather than causing us to stumble, our unHIPP moments can serve us.*

---

voice is really only trying to save me from the fear of stepping out of my comfort zone. It's afraid that I'll put myself out there, and that, *heaven forbid*, you'll discover all my imperfections.

So here's the disclaimer: I am not perfect, and I'm grateful for that. I am, however, committed to making the most of my life and to helping you make the most of yours. As I think about what I can offer you in terms of helping you live your HIPP life, I know I must be transparent and show you every side of me: the dynamo who focuses and gets things done; the Lucille Ball in me who juggles too much and occasionally forgets that a ball is still in the air; the girl who questions herself; and the woman who knows she already has everything she needs inside her.

As I began my writing journey, I felt so incredibly grateful for my HIPP life. I am blessed with a wonderful marriage, a beautiful family, a great business, dear friends, and a zest for life. And as I dug in deeper into what it means to be HIPP, I realized my HIPP life also includes the parts of me that I don't like, the parts of me that I want to hide, forget about, or cover up. Even though life is good, it is not without challenges. In fact, it can be downright hard at times. But I've learned that, rather than causing us to stumble, our *un*HIPP moments can serve us. They can prepare us and help us grow.

All of our experiences—the successes we enjoy *and* the challenges we endure—can help us become our best, HIPP selves. That's why I'm stepping out of my comfort zone and opening my life to you through this book and my blog. To be honest, I would be more comfortable staying under the radar, living my life as a wife, mom, small-business owner, and yogi. But I believe God has placed more on my heart, and His gentle tug has pulled me across the line of comfort. I know He has given me a voice, experience that needs to be shared, and a heart that desires to inspire others. I know He created me to do more than sit back and enjoy my comfortable, and sometimes crazy, life.

At my core I am both a teacher and a student. I am constantly looking for opportunities to grow, learn, share, and mentor. I understand that as much as positive experiences are inspiring, it is our challenges, hardships, and failures that really shape us. The HIPP concept is all well and good; in fact, it is essential, but it is reduced to an ineffectual, pretty bandage unless we acknowledge and learn from the behind-the-scenes struggles we deal with as girls, women, moms, and daughters. In my opinion, we just don't have enough of those conversations because we're too concerned with covering our scars and hiding our flaws. But the reality is, our imperfections make us interesting and our struggles make us stronger!

Everyone faces challenges, and most of us plaster on a smile and pretend that everything is *fine*. Rather than risk letting people see us struggle, we grin and bear it, whatever *it* happens to be. Isn't that what modern-day women are supposed to do? And if you think you're the only one dealing with your issue, let me tell you something: You aren't alone. When we risk being transparent and are willing to have honest conversations with other HIPP women, we can learn so much from one another. More importantly, that authenticity allows us to remain true to ourselves. We can help one another through the hard times, and we can celebrate together when we win. It's time to shift our focus from beating down ourselves and others with gossip and unrealistic expectations, and instead, intentionally focus on building each other up. Just imagine how much more self-confidence *every* woman and girl could enjoy; imagine the positive energy and can-do spirit that would surface in all of our lives if we knew that others were standing up for us, even as we stand up for ourselves.

My hope is that *Living HIPP* will inspire you to share your own experiences in a way that empowers others to live HIPP. When you take that risk, you'll discover, as I have, that your HIPP life is made richer when you recognize and bring out the HIPP in others.

# Become Part of the HIPP Generation

The difference between *Living HIPP* and other books about happiness is that it isn't just about you. Ultimately, Living HIPP is about how you show up in the world. It is about how you interact with your family, friends, co-workers, and strangers. The more HIPP you are, the more people you will infect. Believe me, HIPP is contagious and people will want more of what you have. By authentically modeling HIPP behavior, you will bring out the HIPP in others. By spreading your joy and sharing your spirit, you could literally make someone's day. Do you realize there are people out there who need you? They could use your smile and not your frown, complaints, or gripes; they get enough discouragement from the world already!

Don't just strive to live HIPP for your own sake; decide to bring out the HIPP in others. Just imagine what would happen if every woman and teen girl focused on adding more HIPP to her life. What an incredible revolution that would cause in our world! In the chapter titled "HIPP Generation," you'll learn more about the HIPP movement to empower others to stand up for their lives. I hope you'll commit to being part of the HIPP Generation.

# HIPP is a Decision

A revolution can start with one person's decision to change. Living HIPP begins with you making a decision to find the positive, to change or grow, to accept challenges with an open mind, an open heart, grace, and a sense of humor. Living HIPP starts with the commitment to honor where you have been as well as who you are now so you can intentionally create the life you want. It's so basic and yet so true: We all want to be happy, to feel good and special. That feeling is a decision, and it's yours for the making. Your self-worth is not based on others' opinions, comments, behaviors, or insecurities. Only you can define your self-worth. Decide today to own it, create it, and nurture it.

---

*Living HIPP requires that you bravely stand up for yourself, for your family, and for your life.*

---

In this whirlwind life with all its demands, we rarely take time out to plan for our life. We get busy and neglect to act on our great ideas or to make changes that would improve our lives. How many times have you put off making a change because life is simply *too busy* or because *now isn't the right time*?

Maybe you tell yourself you'll find the time and energy when …

… the kids are in school,
… the kids are out of school,
… work isn't so hectic,
… money isn't so tight,
… you're out of debt,
… you get back from vacation,
… or *(fill in the blank)*.

Doesn't it seem that the longer you wait, the busier life gets? *Stuff* rushes in to immediately fill any openings in your schedule. I understand all of this because I, too, have been caught on the hamster-wheel-of-life, racing like crazy, but going nowhere fast.

That's why I say Living HIPP is a decision. Creating the life you want begins with your choices, intention, focus, mindset, faith, and action. It requires that you bravely stand up for yourself, for your family, and for your life. You have a choice. You can choose to live HIPP. You can choose not to be defined by friends, enemies, bosses, bullies or anyone who has a negative impact on your life.

The bottom line is this: You can choose to break through and break free from whatever is holding you back from living your best life. You may be fighting your weight, clutter, stress, work, substances, shopping, spending, perfection, drama, negativity, broken relationships, or self-sabotage. These things are not your problems; they are the result of your problems. It is time to get to the heart of the fear that blocks your path. It's time to replace that fear and to awaken your spirit so you can live your life fully.

Living HIPP is a life-long journey. I have not yet arrived. In fact, I feel as though I have only just begun. If you'll make the decision to join me on this journey of Living HIPP, then you will discover how amazing life can be, despite—and maybe even *because* of—its imperfections.

# Life Happens

*Do you remember that girl with big dreams who knew she could be whatever she wanted to be?*

You were born perfect. The sight of your ten tiny fingers and ten tiny toes brought so much happiness to your parents and family. All they wanted was for you to live a happy and healthy life and for you to grow into the person you are capable of being. I believe you were born with an amazing spirit and the divine assignment of happiness. Every day, that incredible spirit and *courage* within you grew. As a little girl, you were filled with imagination and unlimited potential.

So, what happened to that little girl?

You know the answer: Life happened. You were challenged by external factors that competed with your ability to live your HIPP life. As humans, we unravel even as we grow. We become tainted, swayed, and influenced by every person and experience we encounter. The dreams we imagine as children are either reinforced or diminished by these encounters.

Regrettably, as we transition into adulthood, we cast aside our little-girl dreams.

My little-girl dream was singing, or more accurately, rockin' out on stage. Struggling to keep our balance while we danced like maniacs on my worn out but neat, flowery bedspread, my friend Jackie and I belted out the lyrics of *Fly like an Eagle* into our hairbrush microphones. We dreamed we would one day join Shaun Cassidy on stage in front of thousands of cheering fans. (If the name Shaun Cassidy doesn't ring a bell, think *Teen Beat* and Justin Bieber). Post-

---

## We all wear a little sign that says:
### MAKE ME FEEL SPECIAL.

---

ers of Shaun, the heart-throb rock star, hung on the walls of the bedroom I shared with my two sisters. Performing there in my room, I felt powerful. I had such spirit, gumption, and a voice that needed to be heard. Even if to others it sounded like we were howling with the wolves, in my heart and mind, I was flying like an eagle.

As a child, you probably loved to play and laugh, too. Like Jackie's and mine, your imagination ran wild with the possibilities life held for you. And, as you moved from little girl to teen, you became more and more aware of other people and your relationship to them. You looked up to the people who treated you well, or whose success impressed you. You also instinctively knew who you did not want to be around. You even developed a relationship with yourself.

Over time, your relationships helped shape you. Unwittingly, those relationships, both positive and negative, took priority in your life. Your dreams became less important as you grew more aware of other people's successes, failures, and their expectations of you.

Stop for a moment and think about how you define yourself—and how you allow others to define you. Look at the list of I-statements below and circle those that are true for you. Don't overthink it; just instinctively circle the phrases you think define you right now.

| | |
|---|---|
| I am passionate. | I have big feelings. |
| I am emotional. | I am sentimental. |
| I am steady. | I am a giver. |
| I think deeply. | I am a taker. |
| I love deeply. | I love to explore. |
| I hurt deeply. | I prefer staying home. |
| I like to be alone. | I love to learn. |
| I crave connection. | I love to teach and inspire. |
| I am a visionary. | I need to feel secure. |
| I get overwhelmed. | I want to be taken care of. |
| I get frustrated. | I am an encourager. |
| I am high-energy. | I make people feel special. |
| I love to have fun. | I am great at balancing life. |
| I like people. | I am healthy. |
| I dislike people. | I am confident. |
| I like to entertain | I am vulnerable. |
| I love family. | I am strong. |
| I love home. | I love to laugh. |
| I have a big heart. | I have a good sense of humor. |

Now, take a look at the statements you circled. Be honest: How many did you choose because they felt like the "right" answer? I can look at that list and think: *Every one of those statements is true for me.* But then I wonder how many of those characteristics am I taking on in order to please others, not because someone made me, but because I wanted to be accepted?

What happens when you remove the statements on that list that just sound good, or popular, or important? What happens if you add in your own defining words? Then you're left with your true self. You are beautiful. You are a miracle. If you get rid of all the labels, titles, images, and fears, you'll discover that you are a beautiful being who has so much to offer this world.

I find this fascinating because most of us will not admit to what degree our relationships affect our behavior and attitudes. Having worked predominately with women over this past decade, I have realized that most of us yearn for acceptance. We want to feel special and to feel like we are part of something. At the same time we put on our camouflage and strap on our invisible Kevlar® to hide and protect our real selves. We don't want to appear weak and vulnerable. Think about how much we talk about things on the outside. We make comments like: "I love your shoes!" or "What a great necklace!" or "Where did you get your bag?" Those external things grab our attention. But I wonder, as we're noticing those things, are we purposely, if subconsciously, trying to distract others so they don't look beyond our own pretty armor? Instead of only pointing out what's on the outside, let's also notice and compliment one another's HIPP characteristics like generosity, kindness, compassion, and transparency.

I wish someone had written this book years ago, when I was an adolescent, because then, just maybe, I would have chosen to reject much of the thinking that prevented me from becoming my best self. It took me a while, but I finally figured out that we cannot control the people with whom we interact; we cannot change the way people respond to us. We can control only our own thoughts, actions, and reactions. If I'd understood that as a teen, I would not have spent so much time trying to fit in, trying to be like others, or be liked by others. I would have cared far less about pleasing other people and, instead, focused my time and energy on doing what I really wanted to do.

But that's not how things went down. During my teen and young adult years, I worried about what other people thought of me. And even though I was popular and likable, I felt insecure. My heart was broken by so-called friends, mean girls, stupid boys, and thoughtless adults. As a result, the relationship I had with myself changed. I started to believe I wasn't pretty, smart, cool, fun, rich, or worthy *enough*. Over time, I surrounded myself with an invisible shield, and *no one* was allowed in "free of charge." People had to *earn* their way into my life. Even though my heart is now big enough to love millions, back then I chose to grant very few people access to it.

I'm willing to bet you've experienced some of those same feelings. You may expend great energy holding people at arms' length to avoid being hurt. Or perhaps you constantly surround yourself with people and make it your goal to be involved with everyone and everything. For many women, excessive involvement (over-commitment) is the key to feeling accepted, loved, appreciated, and special. A friend of mine says, "We all wear a little sign that says: MAKE ME FEEL

# Do You Bring Out the HIPP in Others?

So many women—and men—have paved the way for my HIPP life. Their encouragement empowered me to stand up for myself to discover what HIPP means to me. Because of their example, I am aware that the way I choose to live my life can help or hinder the people around me. The same is true for you. By living your best life and intentionally lifting people up, you can inspire others to live HIPP.

Your life isn't just about you; it's about how you interact with the world around you. Think about that. How do you interact with the people in your life? What example do you model? What legacy will you pass on to the next generation? Do you:

- Inspire or Insult?
- Love or Loathe?
- Encourage or Discourage?
- Learn or Stagnate / Fester / Atrophy?
- Celebrate or Criticize?
- Edify or Envy?
- Build up or Blame?
- Recognize or Resent?
- Believe or Berate?
- Aspire or Attack?
- Compliment or Compare?
- Give or Take?
- Honor or Hurt?

In your HIPP life, it is important to create and take advantage of opportunities to shine your light on others. Inspire others. Love others. Encourage others. Learn from others. Celebrate others. Edify others. Build up others. Recognize others. Believe in others. Compliment others. Give to others. Honor others. What you put into others will come back to you. If you're not feeling loved, give more love. Whatever change you want to see or experience in the world, be that change! Living HIPP isn't about what you have or how much you accomplish in this world. The difference you make in this world is far more important than anything you can do or acquire. Let your spirit be one of light and kindness and love. The more pure, loving, and caring your spirit is, the more you give, share, and bless those around you.

When your spirit is broken, do you look for and find fault with others? Some people harbor so much hurt that they blame others for their own shortcomings to make themselves feel better. Choose to be better than that. Own your life. Refuse to be the "mean girl." Move forward with grace and integrity. Be kind to everyone, *including those who hurt you*. Bless and release them. Rather than devoting your time to changing people, set a HIPP example. Don't allow negative people to change you or dampen your spirit. By living with a spirit of love, and holding on to your belief in your self-worth, even hurtful relationships can make you a stronger, HIPP-er person.

special." It's true! We all want to be accepted, heard, understood, supported, loved, wanted, and respected. That desire stems from a deep, emotional need. The trouble comes when that natural human need is intensified by our relationships or by past experiences we *thought* we had gotten over. When that happens, we set our dreams and goals on the back burner to make room for all the things we think we should do, and be, in order to please others.

---

Girl, you've got to **stop worrying** about what other people think. What other people think is **none of your business.**

---

I know I am not alone. You also may have had dreams fade away because life intervened. Perhaps you had a family or you got busy with work, or both. You took the secure job even though you really wanted to be your own boss. Maybe you ran out of time or money and you settled for less than you really desired. Or, perhaps like me, you feared success and were afraid of what others would think if you dared to step out and go for your dreams. The little voice in your head said, *"Who do you think you are? You don't deserve that kind of joy, success, money, or fame!"*

It's time to tell that voice to take a hike. It's time to stop living in fear. It's time to stop hiding behind the happy façade, pretending you're satisfied with the *status quo*. Girl, you've got to stop worrying about what other people think. What other people think is *none of your business*. The truth is they're probably thinking about you far less than you think they are! Your business is being true to yourself and reinventing yourself for the next stage of your life, while acknowledging that *you* are enough. You are *whole* just as you are.

Are you ready to take off the mask? Are you ready to get real about what you want? Are you ready to discover which labels might be weighing you down and keeping you from living your best life? If you stop judging yourself and others, and start working toward living your HIPP life, you can stop trying to be the perfect wife, mother, daughter, friend, leader, employee, and volunteer. You can embrace yourself, beautiful imperfections and all! When you accept and honor yourself for who you are—an amazing, empowered woman—you will be able to make decisions and improvements to the parts of your life that aren't working for you—*without beating yourself up*. Likewise, your new-found self-confidence will free you from the need to blame others. As you discover who you truly are, and make brave changes to become your best HIPP self, you will discover even more joy, peace, and space for the most important people in your life, including you!

## Where Do You Want To Be In Five Years?

Years ago, I was asked the question, "Where do you want to be in five years?" Feeling fat, broke, and confused, I thought, *Well, I would like to be skinny, rich, fit in every area of my life, and happy!* At the time, I was tired, with babies at home, and a bit depressed. Day after day, I plastered on a happy face. After all, in addition to my little-girl dream of being a rock star, I'd always wanted to be a mom. I should have been happy, right? There I was in a new home, chasing after my beautiful babies, feeling somewhat unfulfilled. Home and family were what I'd always wanted, but I missed putting my energy into other dreams. I hadn't realized that my passion extended beyond the walls of my home. Hear my heart: I wanted to be able to have both. I wanted to be a mom and wife first, but I also needed some time away from home to build something bigger than myself.

That question, "Where do you want to be in five years?" prompted me to find a solution that would empower me to be both a mom and a rock star, although my definition of rock star had changed. It also made me realize that no one could create my life for me. In that moment, it dawned on me that, if I were to fulfill my purpose and live my truest passion, I had to take charge of what was within my control and rely on my belief that God will take care of the rest.

Even though I wanted to be a singer when I was younger, I did not have, and still don't, a great singing voice. Back then my bed was my stage. Today, my platform comprises my experiences and lessons learned. And from that platform, I want to speak to you and empower you to get back

---

### If you want to "have it all," Don't try to "do it all."

---

in touch with yourself. I want you to know you can "have it all," but that it will require you to not "do it all." That's a truth I have experienced firsthand! I understand where you're coming from, and I want to help you get where you *want* to go. I know what it's like to want to . . .

- work when you want to work.
- tell your boss to shove it.
- live in a nice home and afford nice things.
- have peace in your heart.
- be filled with happiness and a sense of wholeness.
- feel better and be your right size.
- work from home.
- work out when you want to work out.
- live with purpose, feel renewal, experience growth and reinvention.
- be yourself.
- make family and relationships a priority.

I know what it feels like to fold laundry while thinking: *This sucks!* I also know how it feels when you're cleaning the toilet, thinking, *this is not how I wanted to spend my Saturday.* And I know what it feels like when life's chores take over, and you feel like all you do is *work* and *do* and *go.* Then you wake up the next day to start all over again.

I've been there. I've "done it all." But I decided a few years ago to make changes so that I don't have to "do it all." I realized I can *have* a clean house, neatly folded laundry, an organized home office, and still do yoga every day, or I can stay in my PJs for the day if I choose. Yes, I still have to do things I don't want to do, but I intentionally design my day in such a way that I spend it enjoying much of what I do. For example, I love to cook some nights, but I am not the cook every night, and I refuse to be the maid every day. So I decided to get some help. Now, don't start with the excuse: *If I could afford help I would (fill in the blank).* We'll get to the how-tos of that, I promise.

In the meantime, my desire is to help you see that you don't, and *shouldn't*, do it all. Instead of singing, I've chosen to use my voice and passion to inspire you to believe in yourself, to go after your dreams, to realize anything is possible. My dream is to inspire women around the world to be HIPP in their own right. In no way have I "arrived," and the success I have achieved didn't magically appear. I worked, visualized, committed, and created. Some days, maybe even most days, don't go as planned. Sometimes I fall; sometimes I fail. However, I know, without a shadow of a doubt, that I'm doing the right thing by choosing to pursue my purpose and live my passion. I follow my heart's desire. Do you?

Role models like Oprah, Joan Lunden, Tory Johnson, and Rita Davenport, who wrote the foreword for this book, each set an example for me. Women like Donna Johnson, who started a home-based business as a single mom and went on to build an empire earning a six-figure *monthly* income, inspire me. I love how, today, in addition to being a wonderful mom and a successful business owner, Donna funds orphanages around the world.

My friend Cecilia is another example of someone who encourages me daily to live HIPP. Cecilia is a work-at-home mom who is raising a family while living debt-free and financially secure. Her faith and love for others not only drive her business's success, they also motivate her to support a number of worthy causes including raising funds to bring fresh water to villages in Africa.

These women are dedicated to growing and evolving into the strong, purpose-driven, balanced individuals they were meant to become. Through their dedication, perseverance, and courage, they not only improved their families' lifestyles but have touched hundreds, if not thousands, or even millions of people's lives. They are living a HIPP life. Beyond the public good they do, they also work hard on their personal lives, from living fit and healthy, to balancing family and community commitments, to finding time to nurture themselves. They strive, like all HIPP women, to live on their terms. By their example, they inspire me, and so many others, to lead a rich, full life. Yet, even as I respect, learn from, and am inspired by these women, I know I, too, must live on my own terms if I am to fulfill the dreams in *my* heart. I can't circle the I-statements I think will make you like me; I have to be true to myself. To live HIPP, you must do the same.

In the next chapter we'll focus on discovering or rediscovering your dreams. You have a gift like no other person on this earth, and that gift is just waiting to be opened up and shared with the world. Your dreams help reveal that gift.

# (Re-)Discovering Your Dreams

*What do you love to do?*
*What makes your heart sing?*

*Y*ou've got to have dreams! You've got to dream big. Dreaming costs nothing, but not dreaming can cost you everything! Have you taken time lately to think about what you really want? Or have you stopped dreaming and started dreading? Are you busy running on life's hamster wheel—living life based on what is thrown at you?

It doesn't matter if you're a stay-at-home mom, a corporate executive, or an entrepreneur; if your life is directing you—instead of you directing your life—there's a problem.

Ten years ago I was racing on the hamster wheel. I was blinded by my great life. I thought I had every*thing* I wanted. Maybe you feel as I did: stuck. My monotonous life was like the movie *Groundhog Day*. For the most part, life wasn't bad. In fact, there were many truly enjoyable moments. But something was missing.

When I was asked where I wanted to be in five years, my immediate response had to do with *more* and *better*: more money, a better body, more energy, more happiness. You, too, may have a desire to create more. *More* could be anything: time, money, joy, wellness, peace, serenity, laughter, purpose, strategy, or contribution. It's tempting to think that if only you could run faster, work harder, juggle more, you'd eventually arrive and achieve that more-and-better life.

---

## If your life is directing you —instead of you directing your life— there's a problem.

---

But then came the question that changed everything: "If you keep doing what you're doing, where will you be five years from now?" I thought: *Oh no! If I keep doing what I'm doing I will have a dozen kids. Help me!*

The piece missing from my life was a clear vision of my dream. I didn't have a driving passion. I was confused about my purpose. As a little girl I had such big dreams, and to this day, I am still a dreamer. At that point in my life, my dreams were gathering dust while I struggled to live up to what I thought others expected of me and what I pictured for myself. I wanted to be the epitome of the perfect mom who does it all—baking, cleaning, fixing, laughing, loving, teaching—all without breaking a sweat or losing her patience. I embraced the mom dream, although I never managed to live up to those unrealistic expectations. But being a great mom was only part of my dream. Early on, I didn't imagine that I could be a mom *and* pursue my other dreams (once I figured out exactly what I wanted). Nor did I realize I could do so on my own terms.

Let me ask you the same questions: Where do you want to be in five years? If you keep doing what you are doing, what will your life look like five years from now? If you are uncomfortable with your answer to the second question, I have great news: You can change that today. You can decide right now to make small changes each day to create more and better opportunities in your life.

You can start creating the life you want by thinking about what it is that really makes your heart sing. What do you love to do? Whatever your answer is, this is your time to venture, to try, to get uncomfortable, and do what you have always wanted to do. Today is the day to begin your HIPP life. The only person stopping you is you. I know, you are busy and you don't have time. I know there is not enough money. I know there are other conflicts and reasons not to, and perhaps your spouse or family isn't on board. Here is the deal: You can have your excuse, or you can have your dream, but you can't have both. Decide to have the courage to go after your dream.

# Dare To Listen To Your Gut

So what's stopping you? See if any of these statements resonate with you:

*I'm not sure I can do it.*
*I don't think I'm smart enough, good enough, talented enough.*
*I might fail.*
*Others will think less of me if I bomb.*
*Others will desert me if I succeed.*

If you can identify with any of those fears, you aren't alone. A fear of what others would think of me if I failed (or succeeded) almost stopped me from starting my own home-based business. Most people in my life thought it was not a good decision to start something new when I was already a

---

*You can have your excuse,*
*or you can have your dream,*
*but you can't have both.*

---

busy mom. Some people didn't like the industry I was considering. Many people told me a home-based, direct selling business could never work.

I am so glad I didn't listen to those well-meaning people. I am so thankful I listened to my instinct, my gut. Don't get me wrong; I was afraid. I thought, *What if they are right? What if it doesn't work and I totally fail?* Fortunately, I also asked myself, *What if it does work?* Listening to myself, rather than the crowd, changed my life.

In that pivotal moment, I stepped forward in faith and stepped far out of my comfort zone. Had I listened to people who truly did not understand the industry and what it takes to be a successful entrepreneur, I would not have the lifestyle, confidence, and sense of purpose I have today. It would have been easier and more comfortable for me to do something else, something more mainstream and seemingly safe. I am so glad I broke through my fears and insecurities, because doing so led me to a newer and deeper level of understanding of myself and what I truly want.

The decision to start my own business (followed by swift action) changed my family's lifestyle. It empowered me to earn an income that allows us to experience a life I only dreamed about. More importantly, I rediscovered my confidence and learned how to be a strong leader. I almost allowed fear to stop me, but I know now that had I not listened to my gut and taken action, I would have missed out on so much of the goodness life offers. I am so grateful my fear of "hanging out my shingle" was not as strong as my dream to create financial security for my family, and to create passion and purpose for me. Although the decision was out of my comfort zone and success seemed beyond the realm of possibility, my business soon became my vehicle for creating balance, excitement, constant personal growth in my life, in addition to a powerful income stream.

I know firsthand how scary it is to go against the current—to do something different. Thankfully, my experience taught me that fear is only temporary. Once I broke through the fear and took action, I realized I was capable of so much more. Shifting my mindset and focus to what was possible, rather than what might go wrong or what others thought of me, empowered me to take a chance on myself and my dreams. Then a truly amazing thing happened. As I pursued my dream and started living my HIPP life, the people around me began to realize they could live their HIPP life, too.

It takes courage to discover and pursue your dreams; but in the end, your courage is a gift that may help others create *their* HIPP life. When your attitude and actions are aligned with your true purpose, opportunities will appear. You simply have to be courageous enough to step forward and grab hold of those opportunities.

What have you been *thinking* about doing *someday*, but keep putting off? Write down your answer here, and take the first step toward claiming your dream!

_____

_____

_____

_____

You might already be doing what you want to do, but feel guilt, pressure, or conflict between your desires and commitments. The more aligned you are with your true self, the sooner that angst and pressure will dissipate. When you are Living HIPP, feelings of overwhelm, busyness, confusion, regret, and frustration will be replaced with joy, purpose, clarity, energy, and authenticity. And although I've shared my story about how my business helps me pursue my purpose and live HIPP, I want you to know that HIPP isn't only about work. It's about you being a healthy, whole—being connected to who you really are and what you want to do. For some people, Living HIPP may include finding or creating work that empowers them to live the life they want. For others it may mean getting rid of the things, people, habits, and attitudes that don't serve them well. In every case, HIPP means living the life you desire.

## Equipping Yourself For Change

I believe everyone needs to be equipped with not only the vision of what is possible, but also practical guidance on *how* to live her or his best life. In my own journey, I discovered a crossroad between success principles and holistic living, also known as the mind-body connection. Living HIPP bridges these two practices. This blend leads to a life of fulfillment and success, even if you need to discover your pain, hurt, and vulnerability in the process. While creating your HIPP life, you will embrace those areas that pertain to you and make the changes necessary to get the results you want. Many of the changes will be small, but when made

---

## Fear is only temporary.

---

daily, they will help you live HIPP. In the chapters that follow, I'll provide you with a number of practical strategies and tips to help you live your HIPP life. But first, you need to get reacquainted with your true self.

To live your best life and discover what's really inside you, it will be necessary to shed the layers of labels and expectations you've covered yourself with. If not removed, those layers will block you from living an authentic life of joy and purpose. No matter how hard you work, you will work against yourself unless you resolve to grow from within. This process is like turning yourself inside out and shaking off all the stuff that is weighing you down. It isn't easy and those labels don't always peel off with one clean rip. This mandatory part of your HIPP journey will force you to identify the beliefs, attitudes, and habits that are preventing you from getting what you want. The truth is, deep down you already know what's inhibiting your success. It's time to remove the illusions, excuses, clutter, negativity, and other *junk* that blocks your path. Listen to your voice, listen

# What's Your Plan B?

If you want more—be it time, money, wellness, joy—you've got to make a change. My change came ten years ago when I decided to launch my home-based business. Little did I know that this one decision would so significantly alter the course of my life.

At the time, I was a stay-at-home mom with three little ones. We had a great home, but I felt a sense of insecurity about our financial future. I didn't just want to be able to pay bills each month, I wanted to create more income, more opportunity, and go from reactive to proactive each month. Like most Americans, we were living paycheck to paycheck, and I knew we weren't prepared for a personal financial disaster. We needed a Plan B.

Becoming self-employed was my solution to taking charge of both my life and my income. One month after I launched my business, my husband was laid off from his professional corporate job. My business, our Plan B, took on new meaning. I was motivated more than ever to succeed. It did not happen overnight, but I made a firm commitment to myself that I would do everything that I could to succeed. With patience, persistence, and hard work, I eventually created an income that exceeded my husband's professional salary.

My income changed our financial life, and my business changed me. It was not the business or the products that changed my life, even though they had a positive effect on me and I loved them. The real impact was how the business balanced out my life. It tapped into my passion, dreams, and desires, and gave me a new path from which to explore things beyond the day-to-day activity of life as a mom and wife. It also gave me a community of positive women who were looking to live their HIPP life.

My Plan B gave me emotional power to own my life, and offered me the earning power to enrich my family's lifestyle. Perhaps most importantly, I proved to myself that I can achieve whatever I put my mind to, so long as I commit and take action. This is true for everyone who is willing to step out of her comfort zone and own her life. This can be true for you.

I chose the road less traveled, and started a business. I know some people say our country's economy is down and that this isn't a good time to start something new; but I choose not to believe the naysayers. Actually, this is an incredibly amazing time, filled with opportunity. And I know from personal experience that having earning power fuels your ability to make choices, and gives you options.

So, what's your Plan B?

to your gut, and take action on addressing what needs to change in order for you to shine your light on this world.

Take a minute right now to identify what's been weighing you down so you can deal with it. Be totally honest with yourself here. No one but you has to see your answers, so lay it on the line.

What do you really want in life?

_____

_____

_____

_____

What fear is holding you back?

_____

_____

_____

_____

What do you believe about yourself and your ability to change?

_____

_____

_____

_____

Who makes you feel bad about yourself, and why do you think that is?

_____

_____

_____

_____

What are you only doing because you feel it's expected of you?

_____

_____

_____

_____

_____

_____

What do you want to stop doing?

_____

_____

_____

_____

_____

What personal habits prevent you from living your best life?

_____

_____

_____

_____

_____

_____

_____

Peeling back the layers can hurt. You will have highs and lows as you navigate your way through this process of self-discovery. But there's an upside: Equipped with this honest assessment of yourself, you can create a mindset that allows you to experience more of what you want in your life. You can go from *re*active to *pro*active. You can jump off that hamster wheel and take your life in a new, HIPP direction.

## Commit To Change

My goal in writing this book is to help you see that *now* is your time. It is your time to create the life you want. It is your time to focus inward so that you can fully enjoy the things and people around you, and release them if they do not serve you. It is your time to step out of your comfort zone. Stop worrying about what others think and realize you are *enough.* You already have everything you need within you to grow and become what you really want.

Sure, it will require courage, sacrifice, hard work, and

commitment to create the life you want. You will have to be true to yourself. You will have to be determined not to live life for other people, so you can live for yourself. But I believe you can do it!

I know as you read this you may be thinking: *Yes, but I have responsibilities for other people.* Maybe you are a mom, wife, daughter, sister, or caretaker. There's no getting around the fact that as women we are responsible for other people. But those responsibilities don't negate your need to discover yourself and your *true* purpose. Instead, let your responsibilities for others drive you to make the changes that allow you to be your best self. The people you love and who love you *want* you to be your best. They *need* that from you. Don't use your responsibilities as excuses not to become the person you were born to be.

When considering where you want to be in the next five years, remember: Where there is a will, there is always a way. Stretch your vision. Know that the sky is truly the limit; that is, unless *you* choose to limit your hopes and dreams. Your mindset is extremely important here. You'll get what you expect. So my recommendation is that you open your heart and mind to the possibilities available to you. Remember: What you think about, you bring about. If you've been limiting yourself, you will need to change your thinking in order to change your life.

So, let's just say, for argument's sake, that you are committed to living your best, most authentic, HIPP life. Does that mean you'll never screw up? Will you live HIPP 100 percent of the time? No way! Living HIPP isn't about perfection. It's about making choices every day that are aligned with your core self, with your dreams and passions. Sometimes you'll make the wrong choices. Some days you'll be hit with one distraction after another. You'll get off track, stuck, and frustrated. But that's *okay*. Living HIPP is not about never falling down; it's about getting back up!

We need to get upset, we need to get stuck, and we need disappointments and challenges. After all, you can't appreciate the sun if you've never seen the rain, right? Adversity leads us to opportunity and understanding. Any successful person will share this truth with you. My mentor reminds me that the people at the top are the biggest losers! That sounds ironic, but it's true. The people at the top in business have failed and been rejected more than their less-successful peers. Top athletes have struck out and lost more games than most people ever play. A-list celebrities tried and failed countless times before they got their big break.

What separates the success stories from the sad stories is a NO-MATTER-WHAT commitment. The people who win big get back up, even after they have fallen, over and over again. They focus less on immediate gratification and more on doing the activity required to take them to the top. They do not dwell on the *no,* or the challenges, or on what their friends are doing, or on what business model or product is hot right now. They focus on their goals and the desire behind that goal. They stick with what they said they were going to do, regardless of what people say, regardless of what the economy looks like, regardless of what is happening in their personal lives. Simply put, they make a DECISION, and they embrace that decision until they arrive where they want to be. And, interestingly, the success they achieve often exceeds what they imagined. Here is the deal: Success is not possible only for them; it is also possible for *you*!

# HIPP Tips on Change

- **Decide** what you want.
- **Declare** what you will do. Tell someone who will hold you accountable.
- **Plan.** *Quickly* decide how you will get where you want to go.
- **Write** down your game plan; write down your specific goals.
- **Do the activity.** Whatever you need to do, use laser focus and JUST DO IT.
- **Celebrate** small successes and wins.
- **Take** small, progressive steps. Don't try to take on the world all at once.
- **Think HIPP thoughts.**

## What Will You Choose To Change?

- Do you want to start a business?
- Do you want to get out of debt or save money?
- Do you want to run a marathon?
- Do you want to begin a wellness plan?
- Do you want to get healthy and detox your body and mind?
- Do you want to lose the extra pounds that are weighing you down?

- Do you want to move past only thinking about an idea, and conquer your fear of putting yourself out there?
- Do you want to foster a new relationship: romantic, friendship, or mentor?
- Do you need to end a relationship?
- Do you want to grow and nurture your faith?
- Do you want to create a better state of being so you can live with less mental and physical clutter, and gain more clarity?

Deep inside, you already know what you want more of. I want you to know you can have it if you choose to step forward in faith and take action. I will hold your hand; you are not alone. But you must choose. If you don't choose, you will lose.

There is a lot of good news with this whole choice concept. The fact is, you have choices. You are in control and you decide how you will respond to every part of your day, week, month, and year. Sure, situations will arise that may be out of your control, and that is okay. You can still choose how to react to those circumstances. Let the realization of exactly how much control you have over your life inspire you to make choices that move you toward your dream. Stop allowing others to choose for you. Choose to *own* your HIPP life!

*Choice drives attitude.*
*Choice drives your situation.*
*Choice drives results.*

There are times we make great choices without seeing the results we want. For example, on days when I eat clean, healthy foods and drink plenty of water, I feel good about respecting my body and my health. But those healthy choices don't instantly put me at my goal weight. My body doesn't miraculously change and suddenly look like Kelly Ripa's body. Over time, though, those healthy choices have a cumulative effect. The same is true of any goal. Small, positive steps each day will eventually and inevitably lead us to our desired outcome. In the meantime, we need to be okay with ourselves in the process. Perfection isn't the goal. Simply taking action each day in some way is embracing HIPP living.

Before we close out this chapter, I want you to commit to making the choice to *own* your life. Identify your dream. Take a moment to dream without boundaries. *What do you really want? Where do you want to be in five years? What would you do if you knew you wouldn't fail?* Write your dreams in the space below. Then, identify three goals that aren't so grandiose—things you could accomplish in the next few months—that will move you toward your big dream. Don't limit yourself with excuses. Remember: *You can have your excuse or you can have your dream, but you can't have both.* Choose the dream.

**My Big Dreams Are:** _____

_____

_____

**Goal #1:** _____

_____

**Goal #2:** _____

_____

**Goal #3:** _____

_____

# Cast A Vision
# For Your Life!

*Open your mind.*
*Envision all that's possible for your life.*

In the previous chapter we discussed the importance and power of dreaming. I hope you took a few minutes to write down the dreams you have for your life. Dreaming is healthy; it opens our hearts and minds to what is possible for our lives. What you dream about is who you really are born to be. *Yes, someday my abs will look like Jillian Michaels' and someday I will sit right next to Oprah, sharing my passion, humor, heart, and home. Maybe Joan Lunden can join us, too!*

But we can't stop at dreaming. Dreaming about what we want, and actually going for it, are two separate things. When your dream becomes a vision, or goal, it becomes something you *own* and create, rather than simply a nice idea.

In this chapter we're going to look at how to move beyond dreaming to create a vision for your life. You'll discover how your purpose fits into making your dreams a reality, and we'll review the important role that mentors and peers can play to help you reach your goals. When you finish this chapter, you should be able to identify not only what you want to do, but also why you want to do it, and who can help you.

Vision has always been an important part of my life, and without it, I would not be where I am today. I have used visualization my entire life, even before I knew what it meant to visualize. As a child, I loved spending time in my corner

---

*When your dream becomes a vision, it becomes something you own and create, rather than simply a nice idea.*

---

of the bedroom I shared with my sisters. As the youngest of five kids, my bed and the walls next to it was the one space I could call my own. I loved to decorate it with items and images that represented me. Alongside my posters of Shaun Cassidy, I taped up magazine pictures that inspired me and made me happy.

These images of people I hoped to meet (or to marry, in Shaun's case), things I wanted to have, feelings I wanted to experience, and places I wanted to go helped me visualize my dreams. At the time, I didn't know a thing about "visualization techniques," I just knew I felt happy surrounded by images of the dreams I aspired to. When I think about how many of my childhood dreams are my reality today, I am blown away by the power of visualization. (I didn't marry Shaun Cassidy, but my husband is a rock star in his own right!)

One vision I had for my life was being a mom and enjoying a great life. I actually had a vision, a picture in my mind's eye, of me walking on the beach with my kids while talking on a cell phone for my business. At the time, I didn't know what the business would be, but I knew I would enjoy it, and that it would allow me to work when I wanted to. I also knew it would pay me very well! That pretty much describes my work and life today. I have a flexible business; I create my own hours and am able to work around my family's schedule. I work hard and enjoy what I do, and I am paid very well because of the business model and company I work with.

Living HIPP is the result of three important activities: dreaming, having a vision (a goal), and creating (taking action). I had a dream for a better life. I envisioned and planned for success. And I created results by working hard. Magic only works in the movies. In real life, sometimes you have to *work* more now, so you can *have* more later. This was certainly true for my business. I knew that if I dedicated five years to building a strong business, I could enjoy the life of my dreams. So, I worked consistently, even when I did not want to. I knew what it would take to make my dream a reality, and I chose to act. I didn't evaluate or come up with excuses; that only slows progress and kills momentum. As a result of my dream, vision, and action, I changed my life.

Dream Big! Get a clear vision of what you want, and pay now so you can play later. Plan your work, then work your plan!

## Vision Sees You Through Hard Times

Vision is important because it allows us to hold on to hope when our circumstances look bleak. Without vision we are trapped in what *was* and what *is*, rather than what *could be*.

Vision allows us to keep the end in mind so we can push through seemingly impossible challenges. As you live your HIPP life, you'll find that having a clear vision can help you change your circumstances and ultimately discover your purpose.

A vision can also replace negative feelings of self-doubt or self-pity with greater positive energy, desires, and beliefs about the possibilities open to you. Like quicksand, self-pity and self-doubt will suck you in and trap you in misery. Use your vision like a life-saving rope. Grab hold of it and pull yourself out of that pit of quicksand, hand over hand, inch by inch. When you cast a vision and then take the necessary steps toward that vision, you create progress. Over time, your progress creates fulfillment and purpose. Then, before you know it, you will be moving, growing, evolving, and thriving in the incredible positive energy in your life.

## Turn Your Dream Into A Vision

I grew up in a working-class town halfway between Boston and Cape Cod. Every so often, my family piled into the car and drove out to my Uncle Johnnie's house in a seaside community on the South Shore of Boston. On the drive down Main Street, I admired the landscape and architecture of the quaint, charming New England town, and thought, *Someday I will live in a town like this.* Uncle Johnnie's home was beautiful, and his wife, Judy, epitomized hospitality. She knew how to make everyone feel at home. As I watched her greet guests or host first-class holiday parties, I knew I wanted to follow her gracious example in my own home someday. I stood in the beautiful foyer with my hands on my hips and said, "I am going to own your house someday, Uncle Johnnie." He looked at his wife and said, "I think she will!"

That was lofty thinking for a girl whose circumstances were far less affluent and not very promising. Although our home was rich in common sense and love, we lived near

---

Without vision we are trapped
in what was and what is,
rather than what could be.

---

the poverty level. Surrounded by some of the most caring, thoughtful people in my working-class community, I grew up with a strong work ethic and a love for others. My parents prepared me for the real world by teaching me solid values and giving me unconditional love. However, neither of them went to college, so they didn't stress school work as much as hard work. My dad's serious heart condition prevented him from working, which meant we had no money for college.

A general lack of funds was only part of the reason I wasn't college bound. My high school guidance counselor, a woman who didn't really know me, told me as nicely as she could that I wasn't college material. She didn't understand that intelligence wasn't the issue when it came to my pathetically average grades. She didn't know how bored I was in class, how pointless algebra and biology homework seemed to a girl who wanted to talk about world events and learn how to create real wealth. She didn't see that my young mind was bursting at the seams with ideas and that I was more interested in entertaining my friends in the classroom.

She saw me only as a poor girl who maintained a C average. Her advice was that I should prepare to be a secretary or plan to go right into the workforce after high school. (If you know anything about Boston-area real estate you know that a secretary's salary won't cover the mortgage on a beautiful, colonial home.) That guidance counselor's shortsightedness hit me hard in the belief department. Now, not only was I convinced I couldn't afford college, but suddenly I believed I didn't have what it would take to succeed there. Her opinion was like a red stamp across my heart that read: NOT GOOD ENOUGH.

Still, I had big dreams, and deep in my heart I knew there was more for me in this world. Far from ready for real life, my friend and I hatched a short-lived plan to get cool jobs at Disney World after graduation. (Did I really want to be a princess in a castle? Knowing me, probably. Although, I worried I would get kicked out of the castle for having too much fun and not taking my role seriously.) We talked about how it was a great organization and that we could work our way up. The desire to *do more and be more* shined through as we talked about Disney's Magic Kingdom, where dreams come true. But those plans dissolved when my friend discovered she was pregnant. The end of our princess dreams literally gave birth to a new dream for my friend. I was lost somewhere far less magical.

Without a vision or a plan, I took a job at the AAA headquarters in Massachusetts. For almost a year, I answered emergency calls from a cubical surrounded by people who lived miserably in their circumstances. These bored adults smoked cigarettes at their desks, complained about work, and constantly made comments such as: "another day, another dollar," or "the rich get richer," or "is it Friday, yet?"

I sat there, eighteen years old, thinking: *This sucks. There has to be more to life. Get me out of here!*

AAA is known for helping people when their cars break down; but I felt as if I were broken down. I needed a jump-start to a new life. My dream of the home and lifestyle I desired jolted me into action. But the dream wasn't enough. I also needed a road map and travel directions—a vision—to get me the heck out of there and to a place that would help me grow.

Despite the fear of failing and of not having enough money to live on, I decided to change my circumstances. With help from a friend's father, I applied to a junior college and took the first step toward owning my life. I applied for financial aid and worked my way through school. College opened my world and taught me a few things about myself. I realized how much my family provided me in terms of love, character, and connection—and how lucky I was for that. As an RA, I saw how disconnected and lost so many of the girls in my dorm seemed to be. Sure, they had all the things money could buy—nice clothes, fancy cars— but many of them were missing a strong sense of self, and the assurance that their families would always be there for them. I also learned that I am the only person who is really in charge of me, and that if I don't stand up for myself, no one else will. I still remember standing with my hands on my hips in front of my history professor, Ron Letteiri. He'd given me a grade that I didn't believe I deserved. Rather than complain to the world, I went straight to him to address, and debate, why I thought I deserved a better grade. I believed so passionately in my work and in myself that he ended up changing my grade. To this day, I don't know if I actually deserved a better grade, or if he was impressed by

# Everything Happens For A Reason

Throughout my college career, I went back to AAA during my summer breaks. After graduation, I returned to AAA while I looked for a job in my field.

Bob, the man in the cubical next to me, playfully teased me about working there. He told me to get a real job because I was "too talented to be answering emergency road-side service calls." Seeing my potential, Bob offered to introduce me to his daughter who was a recruiter in Human Resources at a Harvard Teaching Hospital. That introduction led to a new, and much better, job. Years later, I recruited a great guy to work in our office. He set me up on a blind date with the man who is my husband today.

So when I think about the time I spent at AAA, I know it was all part of a greater plan. It wasn't an accident; it was a collision with destiny.

the courageous young girl standing there with her hands on her hips, challenging authority. This vivid memory seems like a foreshadowing of my purpose to teach girls, teens, and women to stand tall with their hands on their hips and Living HIPP in every way.

Standing with you hands on your hips is a natural position of strength. The stance is a physical demonstration of standing up for your vision, beliefs, dreams, and for yourself. It's a stance that communicates your willingness to protect your body, mind, and heart.

I eventually graduated with a Bachelor of Science degree from a four-year college with a 3.87 grade point average. Had I listened to that clueless guidance counselor, I wouldn't have dared to take a chance on myself, and I would not have the life I have today. Going to college was a huge step for me, not because I needed a piece of paper to succeed, but because it allowed me to prove myself to me. I affirmed to myself that I am good enough and smart enough. During that time, I also received a huge dose of belief from my professor Karen Mutch Jones. She saw in me potential that my high school guidance counselor had missed. Karen encouraged me to attend graduate school—and not just any graduate school, but Harvard or Stanford. Her confidence in my ability to succeed in an Ivy League school made me realize I really could be, do, or have whatever I wanted in life. And that red stamp of NOT GOOD ENOUGH slowly began to wear away.

Later I went back to school to earn a Master's Degree. Between a full-time career and working as a waitress on the side to pay my student loans, it took me almost a decade to complete that degree. While it was not immediate, I knew earning my Master's would only help my career and lead to future opportunities. And the experience, as prolonged as it was, reinforced my belief that anything is possible if you decide, commit, and never, ever give up.

Today, as I drive down Main Street in my charming community north of Boston, I realize many of my childhood dreams have come full circle. I dreamed of living in a beautiful home with a happy family, and then I created a goal and a plan to make it happen. What happened between casting that vision and making it a reality for me today? A lot. I made many choices that required me to take risks, step out of my comfort zone, take action, work hard, deal with rejection, and make some sacrifices. Every step, every challenge

---

### What is God whispering to your heart?

---

and success along the way, helped me create the life I enjoy today.

I share this part of my story with you because I know there are things you want. Our journeys might be very different. Going to college may have been part of your master plan all along. But what I want to share here is that at some point in your life, you will find yourself in a situation you want to escape. In fact, you may be at that point in your life right now. Maybe you long for *more*. I want you to follow that desire. Follow that feeling; it is your HIPP life calling you to live it. I believe your longing is God's whisper, His way of revealing His plan for you, encouraging you to do something that will help you live your best life. Looking back, I wonder what my life would be like today if I had not answered that whisper and followed my desire. I certainly would not have the life I enjoy today. I am thankful for the people who poured their love and belief into me. I'm also grateful for the feisty part of me that stood with my hands on my hips thinking, *Screw you, I am going to do it anyway. Just watch me!* when fears, self-doubt, and other people told me I would fail.

What is it that you want to do? What is God whispering to your heart? Could that be your calling? Your true purpose?

# Discovering Your Purpose

You were born with a purpose. Your dreams reveal your purpose. You may already know your purpose and if so, congratulations! Understanding your purpose is a huge step to Living HIPP. Even if you already know your purpose, I encourage you to stay with me here. Let me affirm you where you are. And if you aren't exactly sure what your purpose is, that's okay! You're taking the right steps to learn what you are here on earth to do.

Remember when I said that Living HIPP is about living your beautiful life as you define it? Well, following your dreams and working to create the life you want also helps you discover and define your purpose. We are happiest when we are fulfilling our purpose, so it only makes sense that we can find it by doing what we love.

When I work with women to help them uncover their purposes, I like to start with a few questions. Take some time now to answer them for yourself. Your answers may reveal part of your purpose.

What are you absolutely passionate about?

_____

_____

_____

What gets your blood pumping and your heart racing?

_____

_____

_____

What are your gifts?

_____

_____

_____

What brings you peace of mind and sincere joy?

_____

_____

_____

What feedback do people give you about your talents or skills?

_____

_____

_____

If you had unlimited money and time, how would you spend it?

_____

_____

_____

If you could be anything, what would you choose to be?

_____

_____

_____

What is inside you? Whatever your answer is to that question, know that it was put there for a reason; and once you uncover the reason and take action, you are well on your way to living your purpose and fulfilling your dreams. Forget about all the reasons why it may not make sense. Don't judge, just do. So many people are afraid to live out their purpose because it takes them outside their comfort zone. I understand the fear or hesitation you may have, because I have had the same feelings at different times in my life. The truth is, change and growth are *usually* uncomfortable. If you're uncomfortable, it means you're probably doing something right!

What's in your heart? What crazy idea do you have? What dream have you put aside because of your busy life, your fears, a demanding job, your self-doubt, or other obstacles? Go back to that dream and ask yourself how it aligns with your purpose. In doing so, you may discover exactly what you are meant to do.

Your purpose shifts and enlarges as you grow and experience successes or failures in life. For instance, you already know I wanted to be a singer when I was a little girl. I wanted to entertain people from the stage. As I grew, my dream and my purpose grew. It became less and less about me, and more about others. Today, I believe my purpose in life is to use my life experiences, heart, and humor to help build up and encourage girls and women.

*A note of caution:* It is not uncommon for people to confuse their purpose with their roles. For example, once I became a mom, I thought that because being a mom was my most important role, it was my purpose. What I neglected to realize was that I can be a mom *and* be a shining example to others, not just by being a parent, but by being me, shar-

# Are You Living Purposefully?

Living purposefully is different from living your purpose, but it is important to being HIPP. Intentionality, or making choices to get the results you desire, pushes you forward while creating peace and happiness in your life. Do you want to know if you're living purposefully? Ask yourself these questions throughout your day:

- Is what I'm doing right now helping me accomplish my goals for today?
- Is this the best use of my time and energy?
- Can I delegate this task to someone else so I can focus on something, or someone, more important?
- Is this choice healthy for me?
- Am I choosing this moment, or just dealing with it?

Purposeful living tests us throughout the day and empowers us to make choices that are aligned with our dreams and vision. The choices we make, moment by moment, create our outcome. Choose to live purposefully.

ing my heart, passion, and inspiration. Being a mom is my most important role; it's essential to who I am. At the same time, I'm not a mom exclusively. I have other roles, desires, and passions that help make me who I am. When I pursue

---

*Don't confuse your purpose with your roles.*

---

those desires and passions, I am able to be a better mom for my kids. For me to have true balance and really enjoy my family and my life, I had to go beyond my role and discover my purpose.

It took me quite a few years to discover my true purpose. In fact, I didn't really define my purpose until I started my home-based business. But through the process of building my business, I learned that not only am I meant to be a leader in my company, but I am meant to inspire millions more to live HIPP and to recognize HIPP in others. I'm still pursuing this huge goal, and I know some people think I'm crazy for even trying. I choose not to listen to them. My platform is to be an example of someone going after her dreams, no matter what people threaten or what fears stand in the way.

I want to encourage you to spend time discovering and pursuing your purpose, even if it seems far fetched. Keep moving forward and push through the barriers and self-doubt. And believe me, I understand how those doubts can creep in. I ask myself regularly, *Who am I, a poor girl raised in a working-class family, thinking she can inspire the world?* But my unshakable belief that God put this purpose in my heart for a reason keeps me focused, day after day.

You can press on, too! And if you're struggling with doubt, remember that it's okay to reach out to supportive friends and mentors.

One day not long ago, my friend Cecilia affirmed my dream and vision in a way that made me feel as though God was speaking to me through her. She looked me in the eyes and said, "You have a message, voice, and such passion and belief that need to be shared." I don't know if we even talked about the specifics of my Living HIPP message. What I do know is that her affirmation reassured me that even as I open myself to ridicule, self-doubt, and fear, I am doing the right thing. We all need people to believe in us and encourage us. And when the shoe is on the other foot, be the one who, like Cecilia, stands up for someone else by encouraging and supporting her and others in their HIPP journey.

You were beautifully made. You are intended for greatness, and you were made to share that greatness with others. You are so important to this world. It is critical for you to believe that you have a specific and wonderful purpose. But it isn't always easy to see we are destined for more; that's where partnering with the right mentors comes into play.

## How Mentors Can Help You Live Your Purpose

One of my mentors doesn't even know me. Oprah Winfrey has been my mentor throughout my life. I watched her show every afternoon from my college dorm room. A bag of chips, a can of Coke, and Oprah on TV was bliss for this little girl with big dreams. She inspired me as a professional in my twenties, encouraged me as a mom in my thirties; and now

# HIPP Tips for
# Choosing a Mentor

In today's information-saturated world, life and business coaches crowd every virtual corner. Some offer great advice; others fall into the category of those who can't do, teach. So how do you know who you should trust as your mentor?

- Look for people whose accomplishments and work you admire.
- Make sure he or she is living a life at least as good as the one you want to live. Why follow someone who is worse off than you?
- Consider whether or not the individual has your best interests at heart, not just your wallet.
- Look at the person's success in *life*, not only with money or business, but also with relationships and wellness.
- Consider the person's character and integrity.
- Remember that you don't necessarily have to hire a mentor. I've never paid Oprah or Rita to mentor me; nevertheless, they've had a huge effect on my life and my success.

in my forties, Oprah challenges me to reinvent myself and step out BIG. Her work influenced me to create the HIPP in my life. She has been a cheerleader who spoke to my heart and gave me hope when I was going through the mundane motions of life. Her new chapter with the OWN network mirrors my own desire to take an already great life and turn up the volume, sharpen the focus, and really make a difference in others' lives beyond anything I have done so far.

You may have mentors who touch you deeply although you don't know them personally. Or, your mentors may be like my dear friend Rita Davenport. The first time I heard Rita speak, she was onstage at my company's national conference. As the company president, she poured energy and belief into the home-based business owners in the audience. Although she spoke to two thousand people that day, it felt as though she spoke directly to me. I walked away from that meeting so inspired by her. I could not help but think, *I want to be like her someday. I want to help people discover their greatness.* I've since worked my way to the top of the company and am privileged to have gotten to know this remarkable woman. Today she is a dear friend and an important mentor in my life.

It is so important to find a mentor as you work to discover and live your life's purpose. Your mentor should set an example of success for you to follow. He or she will inspire you to reach beyond what you ever thought possible. Your mentors can help you cast a vision of what you can be; they can help you stand tall when your belief in yourself waivers. And, like Rita has done for me and so many others, your mentor can snap you to attention when you start to doubt your self-worth and purpose. One question Rita asks is: "How dare you not use the gifts God gave you?" How's that for a wake-up call?

If you're lucky to find a mentor with whom you can interact via phone, email, or in person, make sure he or she understands your dreams, vision, and purpose. A great mentor will hold you accountable to what you say you want. Most importantly, your mentor will help you recognize and squash that ugly voice that pipes up and claims you aren't good or deserving enough to achieve the success you desire. Rather than asking you who you think you are to want so much, your mentor will look you in the eyes and say, "How dare you not use the gifts God gave you?"

Mentors aren't just for work. We need mentors for *life.* Who do you know that lives a life that you desire? I know as a mom, there are so many moms in my life and community that encourage me by their example. I learn from them and am inspired by them. That inspiring influence jolts me into taking action and producing more of the behaviors, habits, and outcomes I want in my life.

## S-T-R-E-T-C-H To Live Your Vision

Living HIPP is all about standing tall (even if you're short), standing up for yourself and saying: "Yes, I can." Believing that your dream is possible may require you to stretch outside your comfort zone. You'll have to be bold and brave enough to step forward despite your fears. Know this: If you have big dreams, you will probably be afraid. That's okay! We are all afraid! Even the people you admire the most were once afraid to step out and stand up for their dreams. Feeling fear is part of stepping up.

Often, the people who seem to live fearlessly have experienced the most fear. For some, like Martha Beck, that fear almost stopped them from following their dreams. From stages around the world and through *O Magazine*, among others, Martha empowers people to be their best. Specifically, she teaches people how to conquer their fears. She can teach others how to do that because she's done it herself. At one time, Martha's biggest fear was public speaking, and she did not like to write. She chose to bravely push past her fears. The result: She created a far bigger life for herself than she ever expected she could as a young adult. Today, Martha is an internationally known public speaker and best-selling author. She has touched countless lives. To fulfill her purpose, she had to break through her fears and turn them around to serve her.

---

*If you don't start moving in the direction of your dreams, you'll never get there.*

---

Standing up and stretching to live your vision will be scary, and you might fail. But if you don't try, you are certain to fail. As a hockey mom, I like Wayne Gretzky's famous quote, "You miss 100 percent of the shots you never take." We can only achieve or accomplish if we *try*. We need to continue to stare down our fears and do it anyway, because that is how we reach our God-given purpose and potential.

In the previous chapter I asked you, *What fear has been holding you back?* Reflect on your answer for a moment and then think about what you need to do to push past that fear.

Write down one small step you can take, one choice you can make today to begin to break through your fear.

_____

_____

_____

_____

Choose today to *try.* You may stumble. You may have to start over a few times. That's okay. As John Maxwell says, if you try and fail, at least you're *failing forward.* If you don't start moving in the direction of your dreams, you'll never get there.

## Circumstance Or Choice

My mentor Rita Davenport taught me that success is living life the way you choose. Living HIPP assumes that you want to be successful *and* be happy, inspired, passionate, and peaceful. HIPP people make choices that allow them to change their circumstances. Furthermore, they don't let their circumstances dictate their future, nor do they blame others for anything. Think about how empowering that is! You can choose to live HIPP, to be successful, to take charge of your life, to stand up for yourself and others.

One of my favorite quotes is: "Whether you think you can, or you think you can't, you're right." Henry Ford knew that success is driven by mindset. Work on your mindset, and increase your level of expectancy. Expect to be more, expect to do more, expect to have more, and expect to move forward to a HIPP life! When you do, your positive mindset, coupled with action, will enable you to be, do, and have what you dream and desire.

---

### Are you a victim, or do you choose victory?

---

So many people settle into their circumstances and expect nothing more than what they have. By not choosing a successful, HIPP life, they are by default choosing to be victims of their circumstances. Victims will always find excuses and reasons for staying stuck, digging deeper into debt, gaining weight, avoiding conflict, not asking for what they want in their relationships, and not going for their dreams. Victims even enroll people into their stories—through blame and codependency—to gain support for their sorry, sad, circumstance-driven life.

What about you? Are you a victim, or do you choose victory? I hope you'll choose victorious living!

HIPP people make the choice for victorious living. When you live HIPP, you look beyond your circumstance and expect to create the life that you want, even when it requires patience, persistence, and hard work.

Choice moves you beyond your circumstances. By choosing to live HIPP, you're taking a stand and leading the way for others who desire to climb out of their circumstances. The fact is, we all fall victim to our circumstances at times. We get down, frustrated, or temporarily stuck on our problems. Those who choose victory identify those negative thoughts and emotions, and move forward with determination. How do you do that? You listen to yourself each day. You become aware of what you think, say, and do. If your thoughts, words, and actions are not aligned with where you want to go, you simply change them. Okay, maybe it's not so simple. Change takes discipline, dedication, and patience. But if you practice and focus on changing your mindset and your level of expectation, your actions will follow suit. Every time you choose victory, you are standing up with your hands on your hips saying, "I deserve more. I deserve better!"

Choice is the killer secret to Living HIPP. Choose victory, choose to step outside your comfort zone, and choose to grow each and every day. And in the meantime, believe that your situation or circumstances do not dictate your outcome. *You* do!

In the next section, you'll discover what it means from a practical standpoint to live Happy, Inspired, Passionate, and Peaceful. You'll also learn *how* to make those words part of your busy, full life on a daily basis. Remember, Living HIPP is NOT about being perfect. Thank goodness! It's about living the life you want and encouraging others to do the same. Living HIPP doesn't mean life suddenly goes exactly as planned. Believe me, there will still be plenty of chaotic moments; but you'll be better equipped to handle those moments. You'll even learn a few tricks for minimizing the chaos so you can enjoy life fully, rather than frantically. Sound good? Then keep reading.

# HIPP TIPS FOR CASTING YOUR VISION

Spend time visualizing your best life. Describe in detail:

- your home and surroundings.
- your city.
- the food you enjoy, and who cooks it!
- who you spend time with.
- the clothes you wear.
- how you feel.
- the vacations you take.
- the work you do.
- what you do in your free time.
- how much you earn.
- how much you give to charities.

## MY VISION FOR MY HIPP LIFE

_____

_____

_____

_____

_____

# Live Happy

*"Most folks are about as happy
as they make up their minds to be."*
~Abraham Lincoln

*Y*ou already know that Living HIPP is a choice, but can you really choose to be happy? Sure, life can be fun; it can also be extremely frustrating. How can you be happy when the house is a wreck and your in-laws are due to arrive in twenty minutes? Or when the dog throws up in the car an hour into a four-hour trek across the state. Or when you have so much to do that you don't even have time to grab a sandwich for lunch. Or when you hear that a "friend" is gossiping about you behind your back. I would argue that on most days, feeling happy is a challenge. So what's the secret to happiness? Choice. How we choose to live makes all the difference.

If you were to evaluate your level of happiness each day, it might depress you. Don't worry; you aren't alone. If you could see me when my kids leave a mess in the house... ain't nobody happy then! But believe it or not, happiness is within us even when we get mad or frustrated or tired. The key to living happy is in our response to the situations that set us off. It is possible to turn those situations and our emotions around. In fact, in almost every circumstance we can choose to take charge and to laugh, fix, or be grateful. When my kids make a mess, I remind myself that I'm grateful to have them!

# Defining Happiness

Before we go any further, let's define what happiness is, and is not. Happy is not a fake, Pollyanna, grin-and-bear-it attitude. Being happy doesn't mean you spend every moment jumping for joy because the world is perfect. Far from it! Almost every day I experience some sort of fear, anger, resentment, or frustration. I bet you do, too. But that doesn't preclude your being happy.

Happiness is living in gratitude and celebrating the life you live, and living your life the way you choose. *Happy* is looking for the opportunity as opposed to the problem. It

---

## Happiness is living your life the way you choose.

---

is seeing the best in a situation as opposed to expecting the worst. *Happy* is realizing you have control over your life. If you are expecting external factors such as other people or circumstances to make you happy, you'll be disappointed. True happiness comes from within. It is only when you peel off those labels and remove the mask and determine to *live authentically* that you can experience true, enduring happiness.

The following questions will help you begin to define happiness for yourself.

What does happiness mean to you?

_____

_____

_____

_____

_____

What brings you joy?

_____

_____

_____

_____

_____

Think of someone you know who lives a happy life. What is it about them or their life that you would like to emulate?

_____

_____

_____

_____

_____

# Take Responsibility For Your Happiness

Putting out fires all day, or dealing with grumpy people can make it hard to see the upside of life. That's when you have a choice to make. You can either give those situations and people control over you and allow them to make you unhappy, or you can laugh it off and remind yourself that happiness is a decision, not a destination. When you are not feeling so happy, or when life is frustrating, that is okay. Acknowledge those feelings and move forward. Try not to be so hard on yourself or others by expecting perfection.

Jack Canfield explained in his book *Success Principles* (HarperCollins) that all of life is a choice. He says:

> If you *want to create the life of your dreams, then you are going to have to take 100% responsibility for your life as well. That means giving up all your victim stories, all the reasons why you can't and why you haven't up until now, and all your blaming of outside circumstances.*
>
> *You have to take the position that you have always had the power to make it different, to get it right, to produce the desired result.*

What if you took 100 percent responsibility for your happiness? Think about how often you place blame or make excuses for why you're unhappy. Consider this:

- Blaming others is a *choice*; so choose not to blame others for your bad attitude or rotten mood. Instead, find something—anything!—about the situation to be grateful for. Force yourself to name at least one positive attribute of the person who is trying to cause you grief.

- Excuses for why you are not where you want to be are exactly that: excuses. Choose not to use excuses. Instead, make a plan and take a positive step toward your goal.
- Holding on to guilt and beating yourself up for past mistakes is also a choice that can make you unhappy. Instead, choose to be kind and forgiving of yourself.

Blaming others and making excuses can make us feel safe or validated. We think those tactics buy us time, but to the contrary, they rob us of the life we were meant to live by preventing us from moving forward.

Holding on to guilt keeps us from grabbing hold of our true potential. Poet Maya Angelou describes the necessity of self-forgiveness this way:

> It is very important for every human being to forgive herself or himself because if you live, you will make mistakes—it is inevitable. But once you do and you see the mistake, then you forgive yourself and say, "Well, if I'd known better I'd have done better," that's all. So you say to people who you think you may have injured, "I'm sorry," and then you say to yourself, "I'm sorry." If we all hold on to the mistake, we can't see our own glory in the mirror because we have the mistake between our faces and the mirror; we can't see what we're capable of being.

The past is like a cancelled check. Accept, forgive, and move on with grace, hope, humility, and humor.

Taking 100 percent responsibility for your past, present, and future is essential to Living HIPP. When you decide to take responsibility for yourself and choose to focus on opportunity rather than obstacles, you open the door to Living HIPP! By making this choice to live HIPP, you influence the world around you, and you inspire others to do the same.

What (or who) are you allowing to rob your happiness?

_____

_____

_____

_____

_____

_____

_____

_____

What can you do to take 100 percent responsibility and reclaim your happiness?

_____

_____

_____

_____

_____

_____

_____

# What's Your Perspective?

There are some days I get so busy juggling, trying to do it all, I don't want to be happy; I want to punch something. Sometimes I even feel like punching happy people in my life because they're so dang happy! Do you ever feel like that? Or, do you put off happiness and say: "I will be happy when I am (_fill in the blank_)"? I know in the past I've thought: _When I reach this goal, or that weight, or this benchmark, then I will be really happy._

Some days, other people trigger unhappiness in my life. In her book, _Life Would Be Easy, If It Weren't for Other People_, Connie Podesta says, "Most of the problems and stress people experience involve other people with whom communication is not easy." Ain't it the truth? Even though I _love_ working with people, sometimes I just can't stand them! While most people are great; some are hard to deal with. Do you know anyone who fits that description?

Life isn't easy. People aren't perfect. Some days are just plain hard. But I have learned, and continue to remind myself: I cannot control other people. I can only control my re-

---

The past is like a cancelled check. Accept, forgive, and move on with grace, hope, humility, and humor.

---

sponse to them. I may not be able to control the traffic that slows me down when I have a million things to do, but I can control my attitude. I can choose not to spend my precious energy and life on garbage thinking. I can choose to find humor in the situation. I can choose gratitude over griping. I can choose to leave the garbage at the curb rather than dragging it through the house.

If you struggle with feeling grateful or laughing when you're frustrated, here is a reminder my mom shared with me: *It could always be worse.* Putting your situation in perspective can influence how you react to a stressful or irritating situation. Learn to appreciate what is, rather than look for what is not there. Sure, at times, things can be ugly; we just don't need to complain about it.

List eight things you are grateful for right now:

1. _____

2. _____

3. _____

4. _____

5. _____

6. _____

7. _____

8. _____

## Attitude of Gratitude

"Gratitude unlocks the fullness of life. It turns what we have into enough, and more. It turns denial into acceptance, chaos to order, confusion to clarity. It can turn a meal into a feast, a house into a home, a stranger into a friend. Gratitude makes sense of our past, brings peace for today, and creates a vision for tomorrow."

—Melody Beattie

## Sharing Happiness

Not only do we want to create a happy life for ourselves, but we also want to share that within our families, work environments, communities, and peer groups. The way you show up in your daily life can influence the people you love. When your happiness is authentic, it radiates and warms everyone around you.

Do you realize that giving another person a smile or a kind greeting, not only makes their day, it makes yours, too? My parents were excellent role models for this. They both *always* had a smile on their face. They made it a point to make friends and strangers alike feel appreciated, respected, and welcomed. I've learned that the simple act of smiling sets the tone for my day and can make a real difference in someone else's day.

So ask yourself: Do people look at you and think you are a kind, happy person? Do you bless others with your smile? Or do you wear a scowl that makes people wonder what they did wrong? One gal in my yoga class has a perpetual scowl on her face. It has gotten to the point that it drives me crazy! I know, it's yoga; I should be more forgiving. I took on the challenge of trying to get her to smile. I

---

Don't join the scowlers of the world in their effort to bring people down. Choose to build others up.

---

thought: *Maybe I can bring out the HIPP in her and get her to crack a smile.* So far it hasn't worked, but I'll keep trying! (The funny thing is, she's probably looking at me thinking, *That Little Miss Sunshine drives me crazy!*) Even as I do my best to bring out the HIPP in her, I realize that I can only control my own attitude. If she doesn't want to be HIPP, that's on her. The reality is, some people are warmer than others. We just need to keep the warmth in our hearts and try to bring out the best in each other. And if the other person is frosty, let it go. Don't let their lame attitude affect your happiness. Don't join the scowlers of the world in their effort to bring people down. Choose to build others up with a smile or a kind gesture.

# Get Happy

On the next page, you'll see ideas and strategies for creating happiness in your life. We all need help staying positive. Using tools and actions can help you boost your mood and create more happiness day to day. At one time in my life, my happiness came in the form of a nice glass of wine at the end of a stressful day. Over time, I realized that did not serve me because one glass became two. Rather than a treat, it became a habit. Like Maya Angelou said, I know better now, so I do better. For me that means doing small things during the day to help me feel calm, happy, and at peace. My biggest outlet is my yoga mat; nobody's gonna get to me there!

Where is your happy place? Where do you go, physically or mentally, to regain perspective on your life? Why not schedule a little "me time" and visit that place today?

The "HIPP Tips to Create Happiness Every Day" are simple suggestions, but many of them will help you improve your state of mind almost instantly. Try them all and see which ones work best for you. Remember: Happiness is a choice.

# HIPP Tips for Creating

- Take ten to fifteen minutes to meditate or pray, preferably first thing in the morning and again before bedtime.
- Align your actions with the goals you want to accomplish each day.
- Go for a brisk walk outdoors. Fresh air does wonders!
- Spend time in nature: garden, walk the dog, go to the ocean or lake.
- Play music you love and which lifts you up. (See the HIPP Play List.)
- Start a gratitude journal and write in it each day.
- Exercise! Physical activity releases hormones that make you feel happy.
- Read something inspirational each day. If you have to, set the alarm to wake up twenty minutes earlier to make time to read. You will be amazed how it shapes your day.
- Do something each day to help someone.
- Give. Find a charity or event you care about. Share your time and money.
- Send a note of appreciation.
- Feed your body well with whole foods that give you more energy and make you feel lighter and better.

# Happiness Every Day!

- Laugh! This happy stuff is not rocket science; just be yourself and find humor in your day. Don't take yourself too seriously. I try to laugh when things go wrong, which means I am laughing on and off throughout the day.
- Look for the joy in stressful situations. If you can't find joy in the moment, at least try to laugh about it later.
- Be grateful.
- Focus on others rather than yourself.
- Share kindness, not judgment.
- Cut fresh flowers from your garden or buy some at a local market. You deserve beauty in your life!
- Pamper yourself. Care about how you look and feel.
- Do a ten-minute sweep to create a clean, serene space in your home.
- Enjoy the sunshine. Let the rays warm your face for five minutes.
- Dance! Singing and dancing really can do wonders for your mood.
- Smile and say hello to a stranger, watch children playing, help someone.
- Sit still and be calm.

# HIPP Play List

Get your groove going with energizing music. Play your favorite feel-good songs when you're in the car or exercising. Sing your heart out! Great music can boost your mood and can get you "in the zone" of rocking your life. ROCK ON!

*Man! I Feel Like a Woman!*, Shania Twain
*Do You Believe in Magic?*, The Lovin' Spoonful
*I Will Survive*, Gloria Gaynor
*We Are Family*, Sister Sledge
*I'm Every Woman*, Whitney Houston
*Isn't She Lovely*, Stevie Wonder
*The Climb*, Miley Cyrus
*Just Fine*, Mary J. Blige
*The Edge of Glory*, Lady Gaga
*Reach*, Gloria Estefan
*One Girl Revolution*, Superchick
*Superwoman*, Alicia Keys
*Goodbye Ordinary*, MercyMe
*Express Yourself*, Madonna
*Stronger*, Kelly Clarkson
*I Hope You Dance*, Lee Ann Womack
*The Greatest Love of All*, Whitney Houston
*Independent Women*, Destiny's Child
*This is Me*, Demi Lovato

# Heart & Soul Play List

Courtesy of my HIPP girlfriend Amanda... more songs guaranteed to get you moving!

*Universal Child,* Annie Lennox
*These Are Days,* 10,000 Maniacs
*Amazing,* One eskimO
*Let the Light In,* Bob Schneider
*Sexy and I Know It,* LMFAO
*Balancing the World,* Eliot Morris
*All Will Be Well,* The Gabe Dixon Band
*I Was Here,* Lady Antebellum
*We Traveled So Far,* Mary Chapin Carpenter
*Brand New Day,* Trevor Hall
*Dancing with Myself,* The Donnas
*Free,* Steven Moakler
*Soulshine,* Warren Haynes
*Beautiful World,* Colin Hay
*Love Invincible,* Michael Franti
*The Most,* Lori McKenna
*This Is It (Your Soul),* Hothouse Flowers
*Shake It Out,* Florence + the Machine
*In the Morning,* Jack Johnson
*Moves Like Jagger,* Maroon 5

# Live Inspired

*"People often say that motivation doesn't last.*
*Well, neither does bathing.*
*That's why we recommend it daily."*
~Zig Ziglar

Human beings experience two types of inspiration: internal and external. When you are Living HIPP, you will understand what it means to receive and give inspiration.

Internal inspiration comes from your spirit within; it is your heart, your soul, your desires and your self-love. Internally, your spirit manifests feelings, energy, and ideas, which benefit not only you, but the world around you as well. Your spirit, then, can become another person's external inspiration. Your internal inspiration is not based on what you learn or what someone teaches you; rather it is felt. It is an expression of feelings and trusting what you cannot see.

External inspiration comes from the people and places around you. It is the example your mentors or others set for you. External inspiration can also come from an image or scene: a place of beauty or accomplishment that touches you in a way that drives you to take action.

Inspiration leads to growth. Growth means changing, learning, and manifesting what you want in life. And when we ignite our spark of inspiration, anything is possible.

## What Energy Do You Project?

Visualize a room full of people, perhaps at a cocktail party. Sitting in one corner, you see a self-centered, needy person who radiates negativity. This person sucks the life out of anyone within hearing distance. Then, in walks a person with a big smile on her face. People notice her as she enters the room. She is confident, she is pleasant; she focuses on others and demonstrates grace. Her positive energy draws people to her like a magnet. Her very presence inspires and uplifts those she encounters.

Which person are you? What kind of energy do you give off? Do you *breathe on* others or do you *breathe life into* others? When you breathe life into others, you inspire them to live their best life. Isn't that the type of person you want to be?

But before you can inspire others, you must be inspired.

## What Inspires You?

What inspires you? Now give some thought to that. It may be just one or two things or people, or several. It can be something simple or profound, tangible or intangible. It may be something that touches your heart or brings you joy. Inspiration may also be a vision of what is possible for your future or a goal to work toward.

Inspiration is so important to Living HIPP because it fuels our ideas and thoughts, and raises the expectations we have for our lives. It adds excitement and joy to life. It is inside of us and it is all around us. We must seek inspiration and expect to be inspired.

Inspiration can come from witnessing heroic acts and small, kind gestures. Sometimes, reading a biography or watching a documentary inspires us to live bigger, bolder

---

*When you are inspired,
you can't help but inspire others.*

---

lives. Other times our relationship with a person challenges us, in a good way, to make a change in our own lives. Being inspired by others brings out the best in us. It is the opposite of jealousy, envy, or negative feelings that drain us. Inspiration turns feelings of "I wish that were me," into "I'm so inspired by that, I will...."

Inspiration, interestingly enough, is a powerful force that connects people. Did your mom ever tell you: "Choose your friends wisely"? In at least this one instance Mom was right! You become like the people you are around most. That's why it is critical for you to choose to spend your time with people you want to be like. Even if you don't realize it, the attitudes and beliefs of the people you spend the most time with rub off on you. I've noticed that when I travel, I start sounding like my Southern friends—and I'm a Boston girl! Do y'all do that, too? Surround yourself with positive people who inspire you to do more and be more.

When you are inspired, you can't help but inspire others.

# How Do You Inspire Others?

Just as the people who shape your life with their example and attitude, you influence others. So how can you make sure you are inspiring—breathing life into people—rather than dragging them down? You be the best you that you can be; it is that simple!

---

Living HIPP means that when you mess up—and we all mess up!—you just get back on track. It is that simple.

---

Think of yourself as a role model in every area of your life. Scary thought, huh? Pretend for a moment that you are starring in the reality show, *Living HIPP*. Everything you do or say will be recorded as an example for others to follow.

I don't know about you, but that thought makes my stomach tighten. I'm sure I could act HIPP for a little while, but could I sustain it?

The answer is yes. Because Living HIPP means that when you mess up—and we all mess up!—you just get back on track. It is that simple. Blaze a positive path for others to follow by being authentically HIPP. Then realize it is other people's business and choice to become inspired by your example. You just do your part by Living HIPP, and others will follow. And if they don't, stay true to your positive path anyway. Remember, some will, some won't, so what!

# Get Clear On Your Inspiration

What inspires you?

_____

_____

_____

_____

_____

Why does that inspire you?

_____

_____

_____

_____

_____

List the names of people who inspire you and explain why.

_____

_____

_____

_____

_____

What characteristics do you want the people in your life to have?

_____

_____

_____

_____

_____

What are you currently doing to take action on inspiration?

_____

_____

_____

_____

_____

What can you do more of to expose yourself to inspiration?

_____

_____

_____

_____

_____

Who can you connect with that is an example of this?

_____

_____

_____

_____

_____

Who can you inspire, and how?

_____

_____

_____

_____

_____

What will you do today to take action on your inspiration and have it fuel your life, your dreams, and your goals?

_____

_____

_____

_____

_____

# HIPP Tips on Living Inspired

- Identify the feelings that inspire you. Use words, songs, or images that allow you to experience those feelings on a daily basis.
- Do one thing each day that inspires you.
- Listen to songs that encourage you. Sing along. Belt it out!
- Find others who share your inspiration; connect with them regularly.
- List the activities required to achieve your goal and then do the work to make daily progress.
- Live in the moment.
- Share your vision and passion, and help others.
- Identify which work or daily responsibilities inhibit or inspire you.
- List what you can change or delegate to make more space for inspired living.
- Make time for the activities you enjoy doing.
- Block out time on your calendar each day to focus, think, and pray. Choose to stop going through the motions and live with intention instead.
- Create spaces in your home that awaken your senses using words, pictures, art, scents, music, fabrics, etc.
- Make a dream board. Fill it with words and pictures that inspire you.
- Simplify your home. Clean spaces can promote comfort and calmness.

# Turn Motivation Into Momentum

If you want your inspiration to fuel your life and lifestyle and give you a true sense of fulfillment with results, you need to move beyond inspiration to motivation. When inspiration affects your actions, two things happen: You move from inspiration to motivation, and you experience the immediate gratification of taking a positive step.

Motivation occurs when you take action on your inspiration. No one can motivate you but you. Motivation uses inspiration to drive results. You can talk about what you want, you can share your excitement and inspiration with everyone around you, but until you motivate yourself to create, act, or do, all that talk amounts to is a dream, a nice thought or idea. All the dreaming, inspiration, and vision

## Words To Move You

Inspiration can get you to Re-think, and take action! Use these nine "Re-" words as you are motivated by the spark of inspiration.
1. Re-ignite
2. Re-commit
3. Re-invent
4. Re-purpose
5. Re-discover
6. Re-fresh
7. Re-store
8. Re-claim
9. Re-lease

in the world cannot move you from point A to point B. You must take the first step, and then the next. Motivation is the missing link between desire and done. If you don't act on inspiration, you will never experience the life you desire. Put your ideas into action! You will only get results when you jump in with both feet and do whatever it is that you really want to do. JUST DO IT!

With every step you take toward your dream, your motivation will grow. Success leads to success, and your desire to succeed will increase. The greater your motivation and desire, the more consistent your actions will become.

---

*If you don't act on inspiration, you will never experience the life you desire.*

---

And when that happens, you will create real momentum. Momentum is your partner in bringing your vision to life! Momentum, when powered by your desire or your "why," drives you to push through tough spots when your energy and excitement run low. Combine motivation and momentum, and you will have the strength to *do* the necessary work long after you have exhausted your mind, body, and spirit.

> *Inspiration* sparks an idea.
>
> *Motivation* is the activity that fans the flames.
>
> *Momentum* is the fuel that enables you to sustain the necessary activity and energy to see your idea through to completion.

It all starts with inspiration. Choose to be inspired *daily*.

# Living HIPP

# Live Passionate!

*"Passion is energy. Feel the power that
comes from focusing on what excites you."*
*~Oprah Winfrey*

**S**ome people believe that the story of the Georgia woman who lifted a car just high enough for neighbors to extricate her son who was pinned underneath is merely an urban legend. Maybe they're right. But let me ask you: If your children were in mortal danger, what would stop you from doing everything in your power to rescue them? If you're a parent, you know the answer: *nothing would stop you*. Most parents would do *anything* to save their babies, no matter their age. That feeling isn't just love, it is *passion*.

Passion is a form of love so strong nothing can stop it. Passion allows us to see through, over, or around obstacles and challenges; it drives us toward a goal, a cause, or a desired outcome. It provides the energy that sustains momentum and keeps us going when we're faced with discouragement. Like a laser beam, passion provides focus in a world of distractions. Its bright energy zeroes in on what is important to us.

Passion can propel us to do things we thought were impossible. That's because it is the one thing that turns lack of experience into expertise. People with passion make up for lack of experience with action; and while they're taking action, they gain the experience they need and move to top positions of performance. Passion drives us to achieve. If you have passion, you are unstoppable.

How would you like to be unstoppable? With passion, you can be! A HIPP life is a life filled with passion. But just as infatuation is not the same as true love, not all "passions" are created equal.

## Choose Your Passion

You may have heard the phrase, Choose your battles. I believe you should also choose your passions.

I've seen people caught up in so many passions that they lack focus. They get excited about a cause and for a week it's all they can talk about. The next week, they moved on to a new

---

**Passion drives us to achieve. If you have passion you are unstoppable.**

---

hobby, like running. Maybe they decided they wanted to run a marathon. For two weeks they train like nobody's business. By week three, their focus has shifted to a new business opportunity. And on and on it goes. None of those passions are bad or wrong; but to really make an impact on your life, your passion must be *the* thing that drives you.

*A word of caution:* Don't confuse passion with hobbies. A hobby is something you do in your spare time, while passion is something you feel so strongly about that you can't *not* do it.

Your passion is often closely tied to your purpose. Think of it this way: If your purpose is your heart, then your passion is the blood that runs through your veins. Too many days we become numbed by all the projects, hobbies, deadlines, and distractions. If you feel dazed because you're going in too many directions, check to see if you have a pulse! When you clear away all those distractions, you can return to your passion and revive your enthusiasm for life.

# What is Your Passion?

HIPP people are passionate people! Take a moment to think about what you are passionate about and why that passion drives you towards your dreams.

What, not who, do you love?

_____

_____

_____

_____

_____

_____

_____

_____

Why are you passionate about this?

_____

_____

_____

_____

_____

What do you love to do that you could be paid for?

_____

_____

_____

_____

_____

If you could do something other than what you are doing now, what would it be?

_____

_____

_____

_____

_____

Who gets paid to do this?

_____

**Take action:** Contact that person today.

How can you diversify or create an additional income so that you can live out your passion and create profit for it?

_____

_____

_____

_____

_____

_____

_____

How would this fit into your already busy life?

_____

_____

_____

_____

Like inspiration, passion is a gift you can share with others. It is one of those intangible traits that we pass on to others. We can even inspire people with our passion. Passion is magnetic!

# Passionate Productivity

Passion is *what* you want, productivity is *how* you get what you want. Passionate productivity is aspiration plus perspiration—and can potentially lead to profit! When you combine inspiration, passion, and productivity, you get results.

Time management is a huge factor in pursing passions, creating income, or enjoying hobbies, and blending those things into an already busy life. In order to be productive, you need to carve out time and have a plan for what you want to accomplish.

# A HIPP Life Requires Planning

Creating a HIPP life takes planning; work-life balance doesn't just happen.

As a business owner, I'm responsible for determining when and how much I will work. While I'm certainly not an organization expert, I know that my practice of planning, and consistently following my plan, has helped me be successful in my business and personal life.

When I started my home-based business, I developed the habit of blocking out time for work *and play* on my calendar. Ten years later, I still block out my work time, as well as key family times (e.g., church, school activities, hockey practice, dance competitions, etc.) on my calendar each week. Then daily, I break down the activities that need to be done in order to meet my weekly goals. This process requires me to prioritize the activities that lead to business growth and profit. I put aside administrative work, which is necessary but not income-producing, until my off-hours. Aside from prioritizing my activities and creating a workable plan for my day, I also evaluate my results each day. Effective planning allows me to achieve my business goals *and* enjoy life. And because my plan is focused on business-building activities, it serves as a road map that, when followed consistently, eventually leads to the results I want.

If the idea of planning your life in such detail sounds like a bit much, think of how you plan your vacations. How likely are you to wake up one day and say, "Today I'm going on a two-week vacation," then hop in the car without a destination in mind and hope you have fun during the next fourteen days? Not likely. The truth is, most of us plan our vacations with extreme care and detail. We want to make sure we get the most out of that precious time off. First, you decide where you want to go. Then you determine how you are going to get there. You create a detailed itinerary with times, dates, directions, and a route to follow. You buy tickets, make reservations, and call ahead to friends you might want to visit along the way.

---

**Why not create a productivity plan that allows you to maximize your life?**

---

You plan your vacation because you want to maximize your fun. So why not create a productivity plan that allows you to maximize your life? Maybe you don't own a business, so you don't need to plan for profit and growth. You can use this time-management strategy to accomplish anything from work goals to home-improvement projects, to volunteer work, and household management; you can use it to create your *HIPP life plan*.

# HIPP Tips on Productivity

- Know your purpose and your true passion.
- Set yearly, monthly, weekly, and daily goals.
- Use a planner.
- Carve out time to work your plan.
- Prioritize the top five things you want to achieve each day.
- Remove distractions from your work environment.
- Balance your project or work with fun: all work and no play is not fun!
- DVR your favorite show and watch it when you're done working for the day.
- Manage phone conversations by starting with: "I have only a few minutes."
- Turn off e-mail alerts and close social networking sites like Facebook. (Social media can be great; just don't let it suck up your productive time.)
- Take a break to clear your mind.
- Scale down on your to-do list. You cannot be everything and everywhere. Be bold, not busy.
- Find a HIPP buddy. Hold each other accountable for activity, but do so in a HIPP way. No one likes a Debbie Downer; no one likes a Perfect Perky Polly either. Chill on that and show you are real.
- Recognize your achievements.
- Reward yourself; give yourself time to relax after you've worked hard.
- Just be you!

# L*ea*rn, G*row*, G*o*

Another important factor in productivity is ensuring you have the right support and resources. These include your physical workspace, the right support people on your team, effective communication systems, etc. The right support also comes in the form of mentors. To be productive and good at what you do, you must be coachable and willing to learn from others. I have grown as a business leader, not because I am a great business leader, but because I have watched and modeled incredible mentors. Learning from others and having great mentors has helped me grow personally and professionally, and also has increased my productivity level. I love to watch my mentors—or people whose lifestyles I admire— and how they prioritize their time and energy. I watch how people live their values, because, more than learning from people's words, I learn from their behavior.

I find I make more productive use of my time when I evaluate my results. Evaluate where you are and what your results are, as well as your level of satisfaction about how you spend your time. If you are not feeling productive or at peace, implement some HIPP strategies to create what you want.

We can become stale and when that happens, we need to get back our vision—our passion and inspiration—and come up with a plan to be productive. What I love about productivity is that you can change it overnight. If you are not feeling productive, grab a pad of paper or your latest techno gadget and make a plan. Then, take the most important first step and *work your plan*. You've got to roll up your sleeves and *just do it*. That famous Nike® slogan extends well beyond fitness. Just as no one else can do your sit-ups for you, no one else can achieve your life goals for you. You may be able to leverage your time or outsource in some areas, but when it comes to *your* work plan, you just have to buckle down and do it! I'm serious about this idea of daily personal action, because I, too, struggle some days to be productive. I know firsthand that procrastination kills productivity. But I also know from experience how productivity and the results it yields can bring success and joy at work and home.

Decide what you want to accomplish, write out your plan, which can be as simple as a quick list to keep you focused, and then get busy. Don't assess or analyze, just jump in and do the work. You'll be amazed at what you accomplish.

# Be Peaceful

*"Start each day by affirming peaceful, contented and
happy attitudes and your days will tend to
be pleasant and successful."*
~Norman Vincent Peale

If you are practicing the HIPP Tips for living happy, inspired, and passionate, then you don't get peaceful; peaceful gets you! Does that sound too good to be true? Between
the rush and hurry of life, it can be difficult to imagine being peaceful, day in and day out. Is it even possible to live
peace-filled?

I'm a busy mom of three, who balances work, family,
and home; I know life's crazy and that peaceful moments
can be few and far between. As a modern woman, your life
probably already feels pretty full, but not of peace. If you're
like me, your to-do list turns constantly in your head like a
rotisserie chicken, and on each rotation you add a new item,
activity, or idea. Most days are filled with work, errands,
projects, children's and spouse's activities; and don't forget
shopping for groceries and making sure the house, pets and
cars are taken care of. All day long, we put out fires, kiss
boo-boos, win business, and make the people in our lives

feel loved and protected. We take care of everything and everyone except ourselves. When we finally do have a spare moment, rather than put up our feet or spend time doing something we really *want* to do, we play catch up. Sound familiar?

# Take Back Your Life

Remember those labels we discussed back on page 17? The ones we allow others to slap on us, or that we willingly applied in order to feel accepted, loved, important, needed, wanted, praiseworthy, or visible? Each of those labels comes with responsibilities, and in many instances, those responsibilities require pleasing others rather than pleasing ourselves. Once you are accustomed to saying yes to others' needs, wishes, and demands, saying "no" no longer seems like an option. And if you do break pattern and say **no** to a request, you feel as if you're letting someone down.

Here's the good news: you've peeled off those old labels! You're no longer bound to the responsibilities they demanded. Your new, primary job is to take responsibility for your life.

Remember Jack Canfield's philosophy: "If you want to create the life of your dreams, then you are going to have to take 100% responsibility for your life as well." Living HIPP means you no longer have to do what others expect. Instead, you get to do what *you* want. Without question, living on your terms takes bravery and boldness. But the reward—the PEACE—that comes when you live your own definition of HIPP is so worth it! As with happiness, the more authentic your life is, the more peace you feel.

After studying business and success for the past decade, I've learned that people often try too hard to be like others. It can be helpful to listen to and learn from successful people; just be careful not to lose yourself by trying to duplicate their success. When you try to be someone or something

---

*Peace comes when you embrace your purpose in this world, work to achieve your dreams, and create your own version of success.*

---

you're not, frustration is inevitable because your heart and spirit aren't in alignment with your goals and activities. In addition, you're not connecting with people because you're not fully you. Peace comes when you embrace your purpose in this world, work to achieve your dreams, and create your own version of success. Be yourself, because everyone else is taken!

Living *your* HIPP life and going after *your* dreams is the first step toward feeling peaceful. But, Living HIPP doesn't mean you no longer race through hectic days. In fact, you may have such a strong sense of urgency to fulfill your dream that some days you collapse into bed completely exhausted, and excited about doing it all again the next day. This may seem inconsistent, but sometimes the pursuit of happiness can lead to unhappiness. Only in the past few years have I learned the importance of practicing peace *while* pursuing my goals. Even when you feel good about your daily activities and the progress you are making toward your goal, it is critical to slow down for a few minutes each day and let yourself regroup and recharge. Enjoy a quiet moment to sip coffee while watching the sun come up, or go for a walk on a

---

*It's amazing how a little self-care can help you be even more productive and balanced.*

---

beautiful afternoon; take ten minutes to sit on the porch and listen to the birds; relax in your comfy chair with a cup of tea. Let peace come over you and refresh your spirit, mind, and body. It's amazing how a little self-care can help you be even more productive and balanced.

Some days, every single thing that can go wrong will go wrong: the kids will get sick, the dog will escape, the car will break down, an unexpected bill will show up in the mailbox; or the cake you made, or bought, for the school bake sale will take a nosedive out of your ten-year-old's hand onto the pavement on the way to class. Those are the days I want to shout "TAXI" and make my escape!

## Be Nice To Yourself

Life can be stressful, and everyday living is not always a joy. Whether you are dealing with the good stress of working toward a goal, or the negative stress that makes your life look like a comedy of errors, stressful days turn up the volume on that little voice in our heads: *You're not good enough. You'll never finish in time. What kind of mother lets a ten-year-old carry a cake? You should have gotten your big butt out of the car and carried it in yourself. And while we're on the topic, when was the last time you went to a gym?* Negative self-talk and self-sabotage affects you physically, spiritually, and emotionally. It shapes how you see yourself, and, as a result, how others see you as well.

Are your thoughts and feelings in contrast with your desire and vision for your life? Negative self-talk and self-doubt can make you feel like an imposter in your own body. Your vision for yourself is of a strong, capable, happy woman doing and being what she loves. But that little voice inside your head continually points out every mistake, every misstep, and every area where you don't measure up. It also loves to mention others' failings. This equal-opportunity pessimist doesn't believe anyone can ever really be good enough. No wonder mental chatter drains your energy and enthusiasm for life. It sucks!

If you want to be peaceful, you must silence that negative self-talk. It won't happen overnight and it takes work; but would you rather be pessimistic or peaceful? If your vote is peaceful, use the following three practices to regain ownership of your thoughts and outlook on life.

## 1. Don't Compare Yourself to Others

Comparing yourself is a sure way to lose in life. There will always be someone prettier, smarter, wealthier, faster, more talented, more connected, more successful, in better shape, with bigger boobs and a smaller waist. That's when your little voice chimes in and says, "Yeah but, her boobs are fake!" Who cares? Acceptance is the lesson here. It is hard not to judge or compare at times, but learning to accept yourself and other people as-is, sets you free from unfair, unrealistic, and inauthentic expectations. Love other people for who they are and be true to yourself. Don't lose yourself by trying to fit in. Let your life, your friends, and your community fit you!

## 2. Breathe Life into Yourself and Others

It is human nature to look for the flaws. It's easy to point out what's wrong. What if you made a point to look for the best in yourself and the people around you? Imagine how much more powerful our society and world would be if we purposely built others up and encouraged each other to thrive.

Women are amazing and so capable, but we can also be a bit catty. (I know, not *you*.) Catty isn't cool. Catty is just a bad replacement for confidence. When you comment on others in an unflattering way, it's an attempt to divert attention from your shortcomings. How do I know this? I have done it. I try not to be that way, but sometimes I mistake humor or venting for what is truly productive or truly compassionate or kind. And, I am nosy. Yeah, that's right, I am nosy. Not nosy as in butting into people's lives, but nosy as in curious about people and how they behave. For example, if someone I don't know well is rude or insincere, I might ask someone, "What's her deal? Is she having a bad day, or is she just a b****?" That's catty.

We all go there sometimes. But being catty or gossiping does not fit into a HIPP life. Make the decision with me to stop gossiping, to stop pointing out flaws, and to start focusing on bringing out the best in people. It's one thing to laugh *with* people; we all need a good sense of humor! However, it's another thing to laugh *at* them. Feel free to laugh at yourself, but think twice before making a joke at someone else's expense. My kids are great about this. Like anyone else, they sometimes laugh at strange or uncomfortable situations, but never in a mean-spirited way. They are always considerate of other people's feelings and are intentional about being inclusive and friendly. They're known by their coaches and teachers as incredibly funny, kind kids. When I grow up, I want to be like them in that regard!

I know, I know: gossiping is natural for women. They were doing it back in Bible times! Sometimes it feels good. I love both getting the scoop and getting things off my chest, don't you? But it's time to make the choice to discern what

---

**Comparing yourself is a sure way to lose in life.**

---

to say, and what not to say. It's time to be kind-hearted and accepting. Consider that every time you are gossiping about someone, someone else may be gossiping about you. (*Ouch!*)

Attempting to hide our flaws by pointing out others' faults does not work. It's an obvious sign of a self-esteem issue. Rather than make fun of someone, take the high road, —the HIPP road—and either choose to sincerely encourage her, or say nothing at all.

## 3. Surround Yourself with Positive People

I've already mentioned that your circle of friends shapes you, whether you're aware of their effect or not. Women who put down others to make themselves look and feel better have a streak of "mean girl" in them. I have a low tolerance for mean girls, and I am sure you do, too. I've chosen to purge them from my life. I encourage you to do the same. Kick the mean girls, the back-stabbers, and "frenemies" out of your life.

If you are surrounded by negative people who think they are better than you or that they "know it all," it's time to move on. Find people who are open, compassionate, and confident in their own skin. And when you find those positive, uplifting friends, let them know how much you appreciate their influence in your life. Send them a note, a gift, or flowers. You may or may not be close to those individuals, but letting them know they inspire you is a gift you give back to them.

## Practicing Peace

A few years ago, I hit some turbulence in my business. Although ups and downs are normal in business, I felt the opposite of peaceful; I felt fearful and uncertain. The more fearful I felt, the worse things got. That's when I made a decision that changed everything. I decided to stay my course and stick with my business *no matter what*. I stopped guessing and complaining, and I dedicated myself to taking care of those things that were in my control. I let go and stopped trying to control things that weren't within my power. I decided to trust that I was where I was supposed to be. Suddenly, peace flooded in and washed away my fear.

When you are feeling challenged, or are struggling with decisions, or are battling negative thoughts, you are not living a life of peace. If you are pushing too hard for something, you are not living a life of peace. When you allow

---

*Lead yourself with your heart.*
*Learn to trust your instincts.*
*Listen to your gut.*

---

others to control your time and zap your energy with their negativity, that's manipulation, not peace. While it is their responsibility to change their attitude, it is your responsibility to stick to your values and to keep moving forward.

Lead yourself with your heart. Learn to trust your instincts. Listen to your gut. You already have everything you need to thrive. You are better than good; you are great!

*Are the people in your life building you up?*

*Do you love the work you do each day?*

*Are you taking the time to care for yourself?*

*Do you feel at peace, or do you feel angst?*

You know what the answers to these questions should be. It is not always easy to choose the path that leads to peace. It is easy to fall victim to the negative thoughts and drama of others. I know; I've been there! Making hard decisions, is, well, *hard*; but you probably already know in your heart what choice is the right one for you. Devote time to considering your options, pray about the issue, and then *decide*. I know from experience that once you commit to the decision that aligns with your HIPP life, peace will come over you.

Peace takes effort. It takes practice. I make the choice daily to practice peace at work, at home, and on my yoga mat. Through my home-based business and through my yoga practice, I've learned that most of the real work in our lives happens on the inside. When you have big dreams and big ambitions, it can be a challenge to feel peaceful and live in the present. I used to always do, do, do. But I've learned that sometimes all that going and doing can block you from getting to a greater level of understanding yourself and creating a life which supports that. Sometimes you just have to stop and *be*. Being at peace is not about being right; it is not about being perfect. It is about being authentic to who you are, and accepting you for *you* while striving, at your own pace, towards *your* greatness. Peace is being comfortable with yourself, not trying to be anyone else but you. My desire is for more people to be themselves and stop trying to be someone else; that is my wish for you. Peace comes when you are at *your* best, not striving to be *the* best.

# HIPP TIPS TO "Peace Out"

- Make time for quiet moments: just you, a cup of tea, and time to think. Don't do; just be.
- Create beautiful spaces in your home.
- Practice yoga.
- Forgive yourself and others.
- Let go.
- Think before you react.
- Always do your best; not the best, your best.
- Be kind to yourself.
- Treat yourself.
- Pray. Rely on your faith.
- Simplify, scale down, de-clutter.
- Act with integrity.
- Believe the best of people. Be compassionate in conflicts.
- Give.
- Love.
- Be grateful in all things.
- See the beauty in every landscape.
- Know you are enough.
- Laugh.
- Teach peace.
- Breathe deeply.
- Look to your Highest Power for guidance.
- Listen to your inner voice and intuition.
- Be real; be you.
- Be serious about your life, but don't take yourself too seriously.
- Be silly, be goofy, and have fun!

# Clean House

*"No more busy work. No more hiding from success.
Leave time, leave space, to grow."*
~Og Mandino

I don't know about you, but I do not enjoy cleaning my house. I love for my house to be clean, but I don't enjoy the work it takes to get it that way. Homes require regular maintenance, from tackling big jobs like cleaning the gutters, annual de-cluttering, and washing windows, to the everyday chores like doing laundry, sweeping and mopping floors, and dusting. Sometimes you can hire people to help you keep your house in tip-top shape: exterminators, carpet cleaners, and Merry Maids. Some jobs you have to handle yourself. Who else is going to go through your closet and know what fits from one season to the next?

Your home and your life mirror each other. If your home is a mess, your life is probably a bit messy. And many of the chores that need to be done to maintain your home—sorting, discarding, scrubbing, cleaning, and handling with care—are the same tasks required to maintain a healthy, happy life.

Following that analogy a bit further, you probably fill your home with all sorts of stuff. That's part of making a house a home. Bringing in furniture and decorations and hanging pictures you love help you create a comfortable, inviting space. Sometimes things wear out, stop working, or simply lose their usefulness, so you have to get rid of

---

> If you've added things to your life
> that no longer serve you,
> it's time to clear them out.

---

them. If you don't toss out the broken items, but continue to add new stuff... well, that's when someone calls the A&E Network and you end up on the show, *Hoarders!* The same principle holds true for your life. A vibrant life is filled with habits, memories, beliefs, and people that bring you joy. If you've added things to your life that no longer serve you, or if you've outgrown certain habits, beliefs, attitudes, or even people, it's time to clear them out. The goal is to make your life comfortable and enjoyable, and to feel at home with yourself and your body. Doing so requires removing the things or people that take up space in your head or heart without adding value, positive energy, inspiration, enjoyment, love, or peace.

Let's face it: We all want to live our best life, but the reality is, life can be hard. HIPP is a foundation on which to build your life. But as you are building a house, sometimes junk—dirt, grime, trash—finds its way in, and mold can get trapped between the walls. The rooms may be beautifully painted and decorated, but that junk is always there. Sometimes junk—such as outdated machines, tax documents from twenty years ago, the ugly bridesmaid's dresses you wore once and know you will *never* wear again—gets shoved into the attic or basement. It sits there, taking up valuable space and acting as a fire hazard.

Too many people fill their lives with pleasure day to day, but forget to do anything about the pain—that junk between the walls and in storage. Are you one of those people? Your pain may stem from something that happened a very long time ago. You may have thought you were over it. Sometimes you've been dealing with the pain for so long you don't consciously remember it's there, or even *why* it's there. All you know is that you're hurting. As a result, you treat the symptoms, not the cause. And subconsciously, you may also hold yourself back out of fear of being hurt even more.

So, if it's subconscious, how do you find the source? How do you discover if an old pain is the root cause of the HIPP-stealing heartaches and challenges you're dealing with today? Here are a few clues:

- You are in a pattern of doing things that don't serve you.
- You let your circumstances and self-limitations stop you from living your purpose or vision.
- You believe that your situation is your lot in life.
- You are waiting for something to get better, or for something to happen, or end, or change, before you make any changes.

In contrast, when you uncover and expose those old hurts, define them, and really, honestly deal with them, you will stop sabotaging yourself. That's when you can move forward and live each day with the purpose of achieving your dreams, goals, and desires. Living HIPP, like any other sort of life, is not a destination; it is an ongoing journey. You will climb hills, struggle up mountains, and encounter all sorts of crazy twists and turns. Just when you think you've arrived at the top, you will discover there are new mountains to climb. You may find a rest stop, but there will always be more adversity, success, failure, and joy-filled moments for

---

*Your own self-discovery will equip you to help others heal themselves.*

---

you to experience. Your comfort zone will continue to grow; but even so, you'll be pushed out of it again and again.

Ultimately, I believe this journey has a divine purpose: to encourage you to delve inside yourself and address the changes that need to happen so you can grow. In the process, you may discover that your life's purpose is helping others move past similar pain and challenges. Your own self-discovery will equip you to effectively help others heal themselves.

If your life is like your home, and it houses the vision and day-to-day activities that lead to what you want, Living HIPP is essential. You are the gatekeeper. You control what goes in and out of your life. If you're not taking your job as a gatekeeper seriously, change that now. Choose to live in a *clean home*. Create an environment in which you can thrive physically, mentally, spiritually and emotionally. Here are ways you can begin to clean house:

# 1. R*emove* N*egative* P*eople*

Negative people, or those who do not build you up, are like a disease that can poison you. Remove these people from your life. The biggest question I hear is, what if you can't, what if they are family? I suggest a crucial, honest conversation that lets the other person know: "When you do this, it makes me feel like this." If the person doesn't live in your home, it may be possible to simply keep your distance, but realize that if you do not address a problem in a relationship it is unlikely to improve on its own.

# 2. R*eplace* N*egative* T*hinking*

Replace negative thinking with positive self-talk. Read Shad Helmstetter's *What to Say When You Talk to Yourself* for practical advice on how to change your self-talk. Women are often their own worst critics. I believe this negativity is an epidemic that affects most modern-day women. We rarely talk about it because we are supposed to be strong, smart, bold, better; you know: "all that and a bag of chips." The problem is, we eat the whole bag of chips when no one is looking! Then, instead of thinking, *I'm great!* we blast ourselves with thoughts like these: *You are too fat. You are not good enough. You are not pretty enough. You don't know how to dress. You have the worst hair. Your skin has wrinkles. Your house is a mess. Your kids don't listen.*

Do you ever beat yourself up like this? I bet you do. I hope you are not so hard on yourself, but we all criticize ourselves to some degree. Please, stop; love yourself completely. That doesn't mean you have to be satisfied with things the way they are, or that there is no room for improvement. Find humor around the areas you need to improve; let your laughter be an affirmation of acceptance. Then, instead of

---

We are supposed to be "all that and a bag of chips." The problem is, we eat the whole bag of chips when no one is looking!

---

berating yourself, turn it around and say something like this: "You are on your way to looking and feeling your best. You are enough. You are beautiful on the inside and out. You have hair and it is great!"

We all need to fill ourselves up; we need to fortify our minds with positive, energizing thoughts. The most positive and successful people I know practice self-love through positive affirmations. Self-love used to sound so strange to me; it made me uncomfortable. I think in part I resisted affirmations like the one above because I was pretending I had it all together, when actually I was missing this important piece to *peace*. But I chose to listen to and learn from people who were where I wanted to be. So I wrote out my affirmations and read them aloud. What initially seemed awkward became uplifting. I learned that affirmations can set the tone for my day. When I get lazy about saying them, I don't feel as fueled, energized, and focused.

If you are new to affirmations, saying them may feel strange. That's normal! Like anything else, the more you do it, the more comfortable it becomes.

# HIPP Tips for Affirmations

- List your top eight priorities and behaviors concerning your life (health, finances, patience, joy, etc.).
- Identify what you want in those areas.
- Write affirmations in present form "I am."
- Write eight affirmations that fit you and direct you in the way you want to be.
- Keep these with you, read first thing in the morning, and read at night.

## Sample HIPP Girl Affirmations

"I am healthy, strong and at my right size. I make healthy living choices each day."

"I am not only good at what I do, I am great, and I see the great in others."

"I am a kind, loving, patient mom, and make the most of my time with my kids."

"I am at the top of my company, changing lives, and creating new opportunities."

"I am filled with faith, and have peace, comfort, and a loving spirit in my heart."

"I get things done, I am focused, I am productive, and I reach the goals I set."

"I know I have something special inside of me. I am going to radiate that to the world today."

"I move my body; I understand that my mind, body, and spirit are integral to my HIPP life."

"I am HIPP and I am part of the HIPP Generation. I empower those around me."

# Affirmation Challenge

Take a moment to write out your HIPP affirmations now. Come up with eight to be great!

1. _____

2. _____

3. _____

4. _____

5. _____

6. _____

7. _____

8. _____

Choose to breathe life and positive thoughts into yourself. Begin by becoming extremely mindful of your self-talk every day. If you think this is strange, just give me one week where you do not let yourself dwell on negative thoughts about yourself or others. Whether you are thinking about yourself or someone else, turn critical thoughts into positive affirmations. Look for and recognize the good in yourself and in others. The shift you will experience—in your own life, in the way you view others, and in the way others view you—will be incredible. Just try it.

**For one week, replace negative self-talk, sarcasm, and gossip with positive affirmations.**

## 3. Discover Your Habits and Emotions

Bad habits are just that: bad habits! Because we are not perfect beings and playing multiple roles is stressful, we look for a crutch, a vice, or a way to escape the stress, deep pain, boredom, irritability, or anxiety we feel. Thankfully, in this day and age, we know the harm of smoking. If you smoke, please stop! Kick that killer-habit right out the door. Smoking is *not* HIPP. Other bad habits include nail biting, eating mindlessly, overeating, drinking excessively, or any other behavior that may be normal in moderation but doesn't serve you when it is abused. We all do things we wish we

---

*Living HIPP is all about keeping and adding things that improve and support your desired life, and removing the junk.*

---

didn't. Most of the time we don't own up to our bad habits, especially if we believe they're "harmless." What we don't see is that these bad habits often keep us from being who we want to be and from achieving our desires. At the very least they hurt us because our actions aren't in alignment with our desires.

I am not an expert in addiction, and this book is not about that. However, I know what it feels like to be compelled by habitual behaviors—some good, others not so good. It is important to talk about good habits versus habits that border on addiction, because the latter can greatly affect your ability to live HIPP. I believe every person has at least one vice or habit that needs to change. My biggest vice is a daily trip to Starbucks. It's not harmful (although some of my hardcore, health-nut friends might disagree), so I keep trekking back each day. However, other vices I turn to for relaxation, enjoyment, or distraction aren't so harmless. Rather than adding to my life, they detract.

In this section, I want you to consider your own behaviors. I've learned firsthand that when you aren't aware of your habits, your simple vices can turn into compulsions. Become aware of your bad habits. Determine if your go-to

---

**Listen to your body and pay attention to how you feel.**

---

habit or vice is a problem, or if it is something you need to monitor. And keep in mind: If you think it might be a problem, then it is a problem. Own it and address it! I realize this can be an uncomfortable conversation to have with yourself, more so with others, but owning up to your bad habits is important to your ability to live a HIPP life.

I believe we struggle with these behaviors more than we care to admit. To get the conversation started, I'm going to share some of my own struggles, starting with food, a vice I have turned to since my twenties. I love food! I enjoy great, healthy foods, but I also love foods that are not so healthy: ice cream, pizza, and French fries are my downfall. For the record, I think pizza once a week is fine. Ice cream and French fries can be harmless as occasional treats. But I am an emotional eater; I eat when I am happy, bored, sad, or anxious. I go to food for relief. In my own process of self-discovery, I learned that the painful emotions I've been trying to soothe or escape from stemmed from experiences I went through in my teens and twenties: experiences of deep pain, great loss, and rejection that left me feeling empty. I also came to understand that the sudden loss of my father in my twenties affected me more deeply than I realized at the time.

Beyond food is drink. In my twenties, I loved to party. Now, when I say party, I don't mean hardcore, all-night binge sessions. I mean socializing with friends on the weekend while enjoying a few drinks at the bar. When I became a mom in my thirties, the bar-party scene was no longer part of my life; I really had no interest in going back. I transitioned to having wine in the evenings. With three kids born within three years, my days were long. At one point, my glass or two of wine became a "medicinal" ritual to help me relax and chill. Now, in my forties and focused on living HIPP, I realize that particular habit, while not one that most would consider excessive, does not serve me. Interestingly, at the same time, my tolerance changed. Wine no longer had a feel-good effect. I went from laughing about wanting to have my wine at night, to whining that it made me feel off.

Don't get me wrong; I am all for us HIPP girls relaxing or getting together for a glass of wine. Just know it is HIPP to be aware of habits that don't serve you. Listen to your body and pay attention to how you feel. If drinking alcohol is weighing on your health and vitality and hampering your ability to feel and be your best, limit it or remove it. For that matter, if food, drink, shopping—*anything*—leaves you feeling less than great, consider it a warning sign. Evaluate whether or not that vice or habit benefits you. Most likely, it does not.

Whether it is food, alcohol, shopping, drama, bad relationships, spending, negative thinking, your attitude toward others, being a workaholic, or any behavior pattern that might be affecting your HIPP life, here's a good question to ask yourself: *Is this serving me well?* If the answer is no, learn more about the behavior and how you can better address it in your life. So many resources are available to you, from

*If you think it might be a problem, then it is a problem.*

counseling to support groups, to friends and mentors who may have experienced something similar. If this is speaking at all to you, now is the time for you to pay more attention and allow yourself to live your best life; remove things and behaviors that are not serving you. When considering what to put in or on her body, my friend Donna asks herself, "Is this fuel or poison?" What a great way to decide what to eat, drink, think, slather on, wear, or even who to surround yourself with! Only fuel is needed for HIPP people, because we've got miles of HIPPness ahead of us to cover. Living HIPP is all about keeping and adding things that improve and support your desired life, and removing the junk, the *poison*. And, when you do expose yourself to poison, remember to be forgiving and compassionate with yourself. Determine to do better and move forward with intention, mindfulness, and purpose.

Let's face it, some days it can be therapeutic to treat yourself to ice cream. Go ahead, grab a spoon and eat it right out of the carton! However, if the occasional treat turns into a regular craving, or if you turn down other healthy activities to feed your craving, that's a problem to address. I know for myself, those early years of mommyhood when I was so exhausted, eating brought me comfort. Maybe you can relate, or maybe you reach for something else for comfort. These days, I try to eat a well-balanced diet and pay attention to what I put in my body. But I am human, and I am a food junkie! I know they say balance and moderation is key, but when I hear people say, "Just eat in moderation" I think, *Come on now, get real! If I could just do that all the time without thinking about it, then I would not have a problem.* Listen, I know it isn't easy to change bad habits. Don't beat yourself up. Don't stress out when someone who doesn't deal with your issue recommends *moderation.* Instead, determine right now to become mindful of your habits and behaviors. That mindfulness will help you determine the right choice for you.

Own up to your bad habits. What vices do you turn to when you are having a bad day?

_____

_____

_____

_____

_____

_____

Do those things or behaviors serve you? Are they fuel or poison?

_____

_____

How will you stop or limit that activity?

_____

_____

_____

_____

_____

_____

_____

If you need help or support in changing this behavior, where could you go or who could you ask?

_____

_____

_____

_____

_____

What alternative, healthier behavior could you choose in-stead? Could you go for a walk or do yoga when you're stressed, rather than reaching for something to shove in your mouth?

_____

_____

_____

_____

_____

# 4. Discover and Heal Old Pains

When we turn to unhealthy things outside ourselves for re-lief, we are usually looking to fill emptiness, soothe a pain, or comfort a hurt. The question to ask is: What is causing those feelings? As I mentioned earlier, when I began to question why I kept doing things that worked against my desire to live a healthy, HIPP life, I uncovered deep pain in my life, pain I thought I was over long ago. The truth is, I never really dealt with that pain; rather, I buried it deep in my heart.

I have learned a great deal about myself in my forties. Much of that knowledge is the result of therapy: a wonder-ful thing! But I am also able to see myself more clearly be-cause I've learned to stop *doing* all the time, and start *being*. In the past few years, I discovered deep hurts from my ado-lescent years and my twenties buried inside me. Because I never really addressed the hurt as I should have, the deep pain refused to go away. I tried to push it down through:

work, exercise, food, drink, and procrastination. I tried to escape it through planning, building, fixing, succeeding, doing, not doing, smiling, dusting off, showing up, canceling, and so on. In addition to that pain, I also buried my desire to be more, do more, and have more in my life. I knew in my heart and head that I wanted more, that I was created for more, but subconscious blocks kept me from achieving more.

I know I am not unique in this. We all get hurt and try to cover it, move on, and keep going. But until you really deal with that early pain, it will keep sabotaging you. How? Well, consider whether you do any of the following:

- Eat too much, or eat the wrong things.
- Drink to overcome anxiety, fear, or numb a pain.
- Over-schedule yourself, volunteer too much, take on too much, and perhaps hide behind your busy schedule.

Notice that everything I've listed above begins with normal, daily activities. None of these things are problems in and of themselves. It's when we use normal activities to hide from pain, boredom, relationships, etc., that we stop experiencing our best possible life. If you are not living the life you desire, take an honest inventory of your behavior. What do you need to change? Listen, we do all sorts of things to escape or hide our pain, but those things don't serve or help us. I also know some people reading this have experienced more horrific circumstances than I've ever had or could even imagine. I know that compared to some, I have a very blessed life. But remember: life isn't about comparison; it's personal. How each person deals with, or ignores, or hides from her circumstances is unique. Pain is pain. And the way your life's events affect you is unique to you. If you just put on a happy face and ignore your pain, that pain haunts you and keeps you from letting your light shine on the world. We need to be resilient, but in the process we should not ignore things we have gone through. It's imperative that we

---

*Pain doesn't go away if you ignore it. Instead, it haunts you and keeps you from letting your light shine on the world.*

---

be compassionate with our emotions and our inner selves. I'm going to share some of my experiences with the hope that it helps you open up and discover something buried in your heart. If that happens, acknowledge it, forgive yourself and others, and be compassionate so you can move forward, healthy and whole. Also, as you look to bring out the HIPP in others, extend that compassion to them. Look at life through their lens and consider what experiences may have shaped them to this point.

## Mean Girls Suck

You've heard the term *frenemy*: someone who acts like your friend, but really isn't. My own experiences with "mean girls" during my teens had a lasting effect on the way I interact with people. For a long time, those memories scarred my self-esteem and really inhibited my ability to trust people. The funny thing was, I was a popular girl and had many real friends. I was a cheerleader, homecoming queen, and prom queen. But even with those titles, I still felt belittled and left out, as if I weren't good enough when I was around two girls in my group of high school friends. I never admitted how those girls and their passive-aggressive behavior made me feel; I never talked about it. I tried to pretend my feelings weren't really hurt. I tried to swallow the lump in my throat and ignore the anxiety I felt when I was around them. What confused me was that these two girls were nice at times, and then at other times would throw digs and do hurtful things. I chose not to be mean back. My spirit has always been one that doesn't want to hurt anyone's feelings; I never wanted others to feel the way I did. I blamed myself for the way those girls treated me; I figured something must be wrong with me. I never told my parents or teachers how I felt; I was ashamed and embarrassed, so I just kept it all inside.

When I went on to college, I honestly thought I had left those painful experiences in the past. I met some new, amazing, life-long friends, did well in school, and I knew my life was in a much better place than those two girls. I was over them, right? Not really. That hurt was still buried inside. And it resurfaced when I was invited to the wedding of one of the girls a year after we graduated from high school. All of my friends were there, and I was so excited to see them and introduce them to my boyfriend. When we got to the reception, instead of being seated at the table with my friends, we were assigned to a table with complete strangers. I pretended it didn't bother me, but on the inside I was so humiliated, embarrassed, hurt, and sad. I blamed myself for not being more likable. I fought back tears the entire time, drank several beers, went home and cried my eyes out. Today, as

Join the **HIPP Generation** and stand with your hands on your hips against mean-girl behavior. Let's link arms and stand up for one another. If you see bullying behavior, be the voice that puts a stop to it.

a grown woman looking back, I know that mean girl was threatened by my self-confidence. She believed I did not deserve to like myself or enjoy life, and she was determined to put me in my place. I know now that her issues had nothing to do with me, but that didn't keep my sweet, sixteen-year-old heart from being broken by her betrayal and ugliness.

Today, anyone who knows me will tell you I am a cheerleader. I am constantly looking for ways to cheer people on, build them up, and bring out the best in them. Part of the HIPP mission is to help teen girls and women establish a mindset that empowers them to stand up for themselves and not allow others to dump their issues on them. If I ever notice meanness in a person, I confront them. I will not tolerate mean girls, no matter how old they are, period. Those passive-aggressive bullies grow up. You can probably spot them a mile away: the "perfect" moms who look down on the way you're raising your children, the women who will stop at nothing, and claw over anyone, to succeed; the anonymous commenters online who accuse, threaten, and belittle people. These women are always ready with snide or insensitive remarks.

We see bullies on the news, the people who take advantage of others. But we rarely talk about the bullies in our everyday lives—the passive-aggressive people whose less visible behavior wreaks havoc on our emotions. I believe we need to stand together to stop bullying. If someone is dumping her issues on you, don't put up with it! Your job is to surround yourself with other HIPP women whose focus is on building up others, not tearing people down. The good news is, most people are kind and loving. You just need to make sure you find your tribe and kick the mean girls off the island!

## Losing My Dad

A more intense and significant pain for me was the sudden loss of my dad when he was only fifty-five years old. I was twenty-seven and it was the most painful experience of my life. This pain was one I did not need to hide, obviously, and it poured out of me. I greatly mourned the loss of my dad. The sadness was so deep, it actually hurt. My heart ached so badly.

I mourned the loss of my dad, but I didn't address the traumatic experience of the event of his death. My boyfriend and I had been at my parents' home that weekend. Early on Sunday morning, September 11, 1994, my boyfriend flung open the door so violently that the doorknob dented the wall. "Call 911; it's George!" he yelled. Mom and I both picked up the phone to dial; it was the moment we had both feared for longer than I can remember. When we ran to the driveway, we found him sitting between the porch and the car, unconscious. Time and scenes blurred together. Mom tried CPR. A neighbor said, "I don't feel a pulse." Finally, the ambulance arrived and the paramedics loaded him into the back. We followed by car, praying that he would survive. Hours later, my dad passed away in the hospital bed with Mom and five children by his side.

The days that followed were a painful, yet incredible tribute and celebration of Dad's life. My family was a team and it seemed so unreal that our team leader was gone. It took a long, long time to recover from losing my dad. Day after day, my morning commute into Boston was punctuated with tears. After a year of unbearable heartbreak, the pain finally started to subside and life began to stabilize for me again.

Losing a parent is life-altering. Any life loss—a parent, a child, a sibling—means hurt, pain, and emptiness for those left behind. You have to move on, but that pain clings to you. Even today, I am extremely sensitive to people who experience death in their families. My heart goes out to people when they experience loss; I take on their pain and mourn for them. I know how much it hurts. And I know that although we must move on, it is incredibly difficult to do so. I remember being mad at the world for going on as if nothing had happened. Healing takes time. If you've experienced a similar loss, I encourage you to rely on your faith to guide you and to feel the presence of your loved one as an angel in your life.

## Take Time To Find Help And Healing

Our painful experiences, whether they include loss of life, hurt feelings, a lost job, bankruptcy, or health crisis, all leave their mark on our lives. Even after I met and married my husband, started a family, and later, started a business, the pains of my past occasionally resurfaced. I had declared what I wanted, created it, and moved forward in life. But even as I built a new life, the way I interacted with people and the way I dealt with stress and drama were all impacted by the damage, heartache, rage, and anger that I thought I had left in my past. It took serious attention—mindfulness and therapy—to uncover, and then deal with the pain that rose to the surface time and again and kept me from being my best, true self. I just wanted to forget about everything. But I finally realized that by acknowledging, healing, accepting, and even learning from painful experiences, those deep wounds can actually make us stronger.

Are you harboring deep hurts? Do you need to let go of shame? Do you blame yourself or someone from your past for a painful experience? If this resonates with you, address it, talk to someone about it and explore it. If you open up and accept both yourself and whatever it was that hurt you, I believe you will be finally free to live your life in peace. Remember, the past is a canceled check. You don't need to dwell on it; however, sometimes you need to better understand yourself and your experiences so you can truly honor yourself with respect, dignity, and the love you deserve. Love all over yourself! Once you really learn to love yourself, then you will truly be able to give love to others. Love heals everything.

Financial
Independence:
"Don't leave home
without it."

# Own Yourself!

*Do you go with the crowd,*
*or go with your heart?*

Once, following a speaking engagement, a very enthusiastic attendee came up to me and said, "You *own* yourself!" While I was honored by her compliment and appreciated her positive feedback, I couldn't help but think, *If she only knew how scared I was inside!* Thankfully, owning yourself does not mean you are fearless. It simply means you are bold enough to take action. That boldness of action opens the door to transformation.

When you own yourself you take charge of yourself, you believe in yourself, and you have conviction in almost everything that you say and do. You are not swayed by others; instead, you base your decisions on your core values, vision, heart and ethics. Make no mistake: Your resolve will be tested, but those tests are also opportunities to define who you are.

*Do you go with the crowd, or go with your heart?*
I choose to go with my heart.

# Believe In Yourself

It is easy to be distracted by what others do or say. When you own yourself, you stand up for yourself. When others disregard or discount your decision to choose your own path, you will need unwavering belief in yourself. Belief is the gateway to your dreams. As you create your HIPP life, your belief will grow. Over time, you will realize you are *more than enough*: You are great and are meant to share your greatness!

Do you remember the one-week challenge on positive self-talk? Belief can start from within, and it can be fostered by others: mentors and HIPP friends who inspire you to be your best. Be intentional about building your belief in yourself. Direct your thoughts, feed your mind uplifting messages, surround yourself with people and things that encourage you. Above all, learn to love and accept yourself as you are, even as you are working on becoming better.

# Fostering Faith

My belief in myself is greatly influenced by my faith in God. For me, my faith is the foundation of my existence. Having faith is a choice. After making the choice to believe, faith becomes part of who you are. Faith steps in when you need it the most and carries you through seemingly impossible circumstances with peace and comfort. If you already have a strong faith, you know this to be true.

Do you realize it is possible to grow your faith? It is not something you have or you don't. Faith is a journey, a process you work through. But unlike working through a math problem, faith is something you experience and learn with your heart, not your head. It isn't always logical, and that's okay! In fact, I believe sometimes our *logic* blocks us from receiving amazing, spiritual gifts. If faith is hard for you, ease back on the logic. Try not to be critical or skeptical. Sometimes you have to rely on your heart to believe what your head doesn't understand. I'm reminded of a comment Oprah Winfrey made to a celebrity guest who did not consider herself spiritual. Oprah asked, "Do you have love in your heart?" When the guest answered "Yes," Oprah replied, "Then you have spirituality. It is a beginning." If you're feeling less than faith-filled, and you want to build faith and strengthen your spirituality, then open up your

## HIPP Tips for Building Belief in Yourself

- Read something positive for thirty minutes every day.
- Write and read affirmations each day, when you wake up and before you go to bed.
- Talk about your goals. Visualize them and post them around your home and office.
- Encourage others.
- Surround yourself with people who affirm and believe in you.
- Be good to yourself: be kind, be forgiving, and explore self-love.
- Live in the moment.
- Nurture your faith and spirituality.

heart and mind; start with love. Ask God, or your Higher Power, to open your eyes to the gift of faith.

I believe one of the biggest gifts of faith is being able to let go, being able to *not* be in charge of everything. Actually, we are only in charge of ourselves; trying to control anyone or anything else is futile anyway! Case in point: I was upset about something in my business and called a friend to ask her advice. While I was sharing my disappointment with her she said, "Maybe this is God's way of protecting you. Rejection can be protection." She flipped the situation around and reminded me to go deeper in my faith. After speaking with her I felt lighter, empowered by the idea that I don't control the outcome, only my reaction. Faith fills in for fear and disappointments we face on a daily basis. That's a great lesson for us control freaks!

## Own Your New HIPP Life

When you own yourself, you believe in yourself enough to take charge of your life. You bring the proverbial hamster wheel to a screeching halt, step off, and decide what you will do and how you will do it. You make the necessary changes to grow into your HIPP life.

John Maxwell says, "Change is inevitable, growth is optional." To really experience the fullness of life and become who you are meant to be, you must choose to grow. What may have been your big goal five or ten years ago seems like a small accomplishment now. Your expectations have changed, and that's good! Today, a great accomplishment may include experiencing *more* in some areas of your life. It may mean pushing yourself to move forward. Or, if you are on the fast track, your goal may be to slow down and live in the present. As you grow, give thought to what your new HIPP life looks like in terms of how you spend your time and balance your life. Most women I coach struggle with balance. They feel trapped by their schedule, their work, and their finances. They want more time and better results, but their business and commitments leave them with little time to think about how to create a better life. To create balance, you must change the way you spend your time.

As I shared before, balance is not easy or without struggle and juggle. Thankfully, balance and Living HIPP aren't about keeping a scorecard or devoting equal amounts of time to every area of your life. It is about creating the life you want and spending enough time tending to important areas of your life. Most people agree that the following seven areas are critical to a healthy, vibrant, HIPP life:

- Family and Friends
- Relationships
- Faith and Spirituality
- Work and Career
- Health and Wellness
- Finances
- Fun and Leisure

In this section, I'd like you to take a look at each of these areas. We'll just touch on these key components of life here because each topic could be a book on its own! But I want to make you aware of what balance looks like. Are one or more of these areas demanding too much of your time? Are you neglecting any of these critical areas of your life? How can you change that?

## Family and Friends

How much time do you spend with your family? Do you plan your work around your family, or is the opposite true? Is your schedule flexible enough that you are able to spend time with your family whenever you want?

I actually started my direct selling business, not because I like selling (truth be told, I did not want to sell anything), but because I wanted a flexible work schedule and unlimited earning potential. I wanted to work on my *own* terms. Who doesn't want that? My desire for flexibility led me to an entirely new opportunity, and my life changed as a result. Direct selling wasn't my first thought. Be open. You may never have thought about starting your own business or changing careers. However, to have the flexibility you want, you may need to think outside the box.

*Family:* How do you plan for family time? Life is busy, and raising a family is demanding. Sometimes you need to hit the pause button and plan for meaningful time. Does your lifestyle support your mission for your family? Do you spend time regularly with family? For those of you with children, think of ways you can spend quality time with each child.

*Friends:* Friendships are such a gift. Whenever I get together with friends, I am aware that we don't get together often enough. You already know how important it is to choose your friends wisely, but once you've established those good relationships, make time for them. Let your friends know you appreciate them, and be sure to recognize the HIPP in them.

What can you do to adjust your work/life balance to create more time for what you want to do?

_____

_____

_____

_____

_____

_____

_____

_____

Carve out family time on your schedule. Driving the kids everywhere doesn't count! What day or time can you plan for family time this week? What will you do together? Remember it can be as simple as sharing a family meal, taking time to laugh, talk, and share.

_____

_____

_____

_____

_____

_____

_____

# Relationships

Do you make time for your marriage or relationship? Sometimes my husband and I are like ships passing in the night. To adjust to the changes and growth we've seen in our lives, we need to make time for our relationship so we can change and grow *together*.

At the same time, in any relationship you need to maintain your own identity. In our home, my husband and I contribute equally and make decisions jointly based on the needs of the family. I'll bet it doesn't surprise you to know I have a voice in our relationship! In contrast, I have observed some relationships in which the husband or boyfriend makes all the decisions. Wake up HIPP girls! This is not the 1950s. Own yourself! A healthy, unified marriage takes two parties.

Make sure to schedule time to grow as a couple. My husband and I try to have a date night once a week, even if our date is staying in for a nice dinner, conversation, or watching a romantic comedy together. What one thing can you do this week to reconnect with your significant other?

_____

_____

_____

For you single HIPP girls, remember to rely on your gut when it comes to choosing "Mr. Right." If your instincts tell you you're not with the right guy, move on. Your Prince Charming will come; you may just need to kiss a few more frogs.

## Faith and Spirituality

Sometimes owning your faith means letting go. With all the labels and opinions that surround religion and faith, it is important that you know what you believe. Embrace your faith and own it. That doesn't mean you should be critical of others if their beliefs differ from your own. I believe we are called to love each other no matter what. But at the same time, if you don't know what you really believe, you will be swayed by anything that sounds appealing. Get in touch with your spiritual self and own your faith. If you don't know how to do that, get some guidance. Talk to faith-filled people you admire; ask what they believe and what they have done to grow their faith. And, as with any other area of life, you will want to devote time each day to connecting with your faith. This connection truly will take you from breathing to *living*. One thing I do daily to strengthen my faith is read books like Joyce Meyer's devotionals, *Starting Your Day Right* and *Ending Your Day Right*.

What can you do this week to nurture your faith?

_____

_____

_____

_____

Who could you talk to that could help you grow?

_____

_____

Cultivating your spirit is the essence of living well. Start by being open and connecting to your inner voice. If you listen, you'll hear it saying, "The more in alignment we are, the more you will be living out your true purpose." Open yourself to the truth that your spirit already knows. When your mind, body, and spirit are connected, they work together to guide you to living your best life.

## WORK *AND* CAREER

You do not *have to* work for a company; you do not *have to* listen to the boss. If you don't like your work or career situation, change it. Oh, I know, I can already hear the "But...." Here's the deal: There is never a good time to change. Change is almost always a risk, and starting over or starting something new can be scary. Break through and do it anyway. I am blown away by the number of people who just survive day to day doing work they don't enjoy. If you don't love what you do, if you are not following your heart, consider this your opportunity to reinvent yourself. Just do it! Reinvention is a key to living fully. Be open to change that can help you create the personal and professional life you desire.

What skills, behaviors, or qualifications do you need to grow professionally?

---------------------------------------------------------------

---------------------------------------------------------------

---------------------------------------------------------------

What do you need to buy or study to equip yourself?

_____

_____

_____

_____

_____

What network can you become part of that would encourage you, and in which you can learn from others and make connections?

_____

_____

_____

_____

_____

What resources and support do you need such as a website, business cards, etc.?

_____

_____

_____

_____

_____

## Health and Wellness

This is an area that so many of us don't prioritize. These past few years, I chose to make my health and wellness a priority. I made time to take care of myself. I stopped saying, "When *this* happens, then I will...." I'm done with waiting to live better. Today, I choose to live a healthy lifestyle and prioritize my schedule and life to reflect that. Are you making time for your health? Here's the truth: When you take care of your body, you will experience improvements in every other area of your life. Choose to make wellness a daily priority.

What changes do you need to make to improve your health?

_____

_____

_____

_____

_____

How can you incorporate those changes into your daily life?

_____

_____

_____

_____

_____

What are you willing to give up so you can devote more time to exercise?

_____

_____

_____

_____

# Finances

Unless you are in the top one percent of the population, your finances are likely an issue. I believe that to improve the areas of life mentioned above, you will also need to positively impact your bottom line. When you truly own yourself, you take charge of your finances. In my twenties I got into major debt because the lifestyle I wanted cost more, far more, than my meager salary could afford. "Have plastic, will travel" was my mantra as a young woman just out of college.

When I finally realized that digging myself deeper in debt wasn't the solution, I took control of my finances and changed my situation. First I reviewed everything. I listed all my debt and compared it to my income. Then I got a second job to pay off my debt. I stopped pretending I had money to spend. With my new mindfulness about money, I looked at want versus need. I stopped using my credit cards and put myself on a budget. I really never grasped how dangerous credit cards are until I was thousands of dollars in debt. Today, I do not buy anything unless I can pay cash for it. My advice: Stop using and cut up your credit cards.

With a goal and a plan, I got myself out of debt. What can you do to change your financial future? How can you pay down debt? How can you create more income? I've heard Dave Ramsey recommend that people start a home-based business rather than get a second job. I could not agree more; working for yourself allows you to get paid what you are worth!

A major question for women is: Are you financially strong? Are you financially independent? If the answer is "no," what are you going to do about it?

_____

_____

_____

_____

Are you in debt?         YES     NO

If so, list your credit card and consumer debts. Get real about how much you owe.

**Lender**                          **$ Amount**

_____          _____

_____          _____

_____          _____

_____          _____

_____          _____

**Total Debt:** $_____

Create an action plan for getting out of credit card debt. Determine how much you need to pay to eliminate your credit card debt within twelve to twenty-four months. Do you need to find a second source of income to make that happen? Consider how you can create multiple streams of income. Not relying on a single avenue of income is vital to creating financial freedom and security.

## Fun and Leisure

As you are doing all the work to own yourself, be sure to balance it out with some fun. Make time in each day, even if it can only be a few minutes, to do things you enjoy. Carve out time on your calendar each month for fun activities and hobbies you enjoy. The H in HIPP means a Happy life. Be intentional about adding fun and laughter to your life. Do things that make you feel good. Your fun and leisure should not be for anyone but you. Sure, you will have family fun and girlfriend fun, but what fun can you have with yourself? Do you make yourself laugh? Do you see the humor in situations where you just break out in laughter? Do you spend time with fun people? My husband and I laugh so much; humor keeps us sane! Who in your life makes you laugh? Get silly; look for laughs and lighten up!

I have to make myself take fun breaks some days because I get busy just like you. If my brain is spinning and I'm running nonstop, that is a red flag for me to slow down, take a breath, and enjoy some tranquility. Even a warm cup of tea sitting by the window on a cold winter day is great. Sitting outside with the sun beaming on my face while listening to the birds also works well. A few moments of relaxation gives me a surge of joy in the grind of a busy day. Be good to yourself, have fun, pause, and explore the opportunities for fun and leisure around you. My favorite place to go is the beach. Where is your favorite place to relax? Do you make time to go there?

What do you love to do that you haven't done in a while?

_____

_____

_____

_____

Where can you fit that activity into your schedule this week or this month?

_____

_____

# Own Your Day, Own Your Life

Pay attention to how you spend your time. Do your daily activities support your HIPP life? Discern what goes on your calendar. How can you make the months ahead serve your HIPP life? What reinvention do you want to see for yourself?

You've got to stand up tall and own yourself. Accept the humor and craziness of life, and then visualize a picture of what you want in your life. Know you have everything inside of you to create the life you want. *Believe*. When you own your life, you eventually color in that picture. You crown yourself HIPP as you own your world. You go, girl! Color your world. Life is your canvas and you are the artist. There is only one masterpiece like you. Color outside the lines!

# HIPP TIPS TO OWN YOUR LIFE

- Decide to be your own boss.
- Create your income, own your finances... no matter how small.
- Define your core values.
- Decide what legacy you want to leave.
- Be true to yourself.
- Assess your life balance.
- Decide which areas need more attention, then make time on your calendar.
- Write a life mission statement.
- Refresh, renew, plan, and give thought to the life you want.
- Take action!
- Act with integrity even when doing so requires making difficult decisions.
- Don't try to fit in. Stand out. Stand up... with your hands on your hips!
- Have fun!

# Live Well

*"A good laugh and a long sleep are*
*the best cures in the doctor's book."*
~Irish Proverb

**W**ellness is the foundation to HIPP Living. The connection between mind, body, and spirit is really the force of feeling balance in your life. Vitality and empowerment shine from the inside out. Wellness comes from nourishing and conditioning your mind and body. Wellness in mind, body, and spirit creates an amazing synergy that propels a HIPP life.

Wellness covers a variety of things that you can do on a daily or weekly basis to help you look and feel great. Living HIPP is about creating a well-balanced life, one that focuses on the whole being. Even small changes in a healthier direction can be extremely beneficial. These changes should not include punishing yourself with crash diets, painful exercises, or giving up what you enjoy. On the contrary, wellness means nourishing yourself with a bounty of good food to fuel your body, hydrating yourself, and filling your mind with good thoughts and energy. It is not depriving yourself of anything, but caring for yourself and moving in the direction of feeling great. As a result, you will *look* great because beauty comes from the inside out! Let's look at a few of the ways you can improve your wellness.

# Finding Your Healthy Weight

I shared earlier that I've struggled with food since my twenties. Weight gain was a natural consequence of that battle. In college, gaining the "freshmen fifteen" quickly taught me the importance of diet and exercise. However, I didn't always practice what I knew. Can you relate to this? In addition to being an emotional eater, I simply love food! I never miss a meal, snack, or dessert. I am not one of those people who is too busy to eat.

As a bride, I walked down the aisle in shape, at a normal weight for me; I was "Petite Pammy," my right size. Within a year, our daughter was born. Her brothers came along in the next two years. After having three babies in three years, I was not exactly ready for the cover of *Shape Magazine*! Over the course of five years I gained thirty pounds. I felt incredibly "fat" and uncomfortable. I was born with a small frame, so I realize I am not dealing with obesity, BUTT (yes, double tt), those extra pounds weighed me down emotionally, spiritually, and physically! During the past five years I have lost and maintained weight; and finally, this past year I reached my goal weight. It clearly was a decision, a commitment, and *work* to reach that goal. Has it been worth it? Yes! I feel better than I have in more than a decade. I realize now how important being at my right size is to my overall health and wellness.

My healthy weight is a major factor in my ability to live HIPP, and I am sure the same is true for you. In my discovery, I learned that my body has a huge influence on my mind, and when I am not at *my* right size, I feel weighed down in so many areas of my life. I only discovered this because I got back to the weight that I was when I felt good,

---

*Wellness in mind, body, and spirit creates an amazing synergy that propels a HIPP life.*

---

and guess what? I felt incredibly great. I was eating well, working out a lot, and practicing yoga regularly. I thought my abs were gone forever; I thought I forfeited them when I gave birth to my three children. Once I saw the muscle behind the mask, I felt like me again.

I'm not gonna lie: Losing weight isn't easy. The negative self-talk every time I looked in the mirror was disheartening. I learned I had to live with intention; I had to be mindful of almost everything. Making the commitment to eat well and exercise, and then *follow through* was a daily decision. And, just as I mentioned earlier, I had to change that negative self-talk into self-love and accept myself and love my body.

If you're living with excess weight, create an action plan that includes a healthy diet and regular exercise. Losing weight increases confidence. It is also your chance to stop hiding behind the layers of "consumption" that hide who you really are. But getting to your right size is about far more than weight loss; it must start with taking great care of yourself. If you feel vibrant at the weight you are at, that is great! Stay there and don't make any changes unless your doctor tells you to. It is not about being skinny. It is about being comfortable in your own skin.

Sometimes people lose weight and they still don't feel better about themselves because they have not changed inside. Being healthy is not so much about how you look— even though we all want to look good—it is more about how you feel. When you are your "right size," you feel comfortable in your own skin and you own yourself. Pursue your right size with a mindset of forgiveness, peace, and balance. Having a healthy relationship with your body is important; the number on the scale is not! In fact, most experts will tell you to throw your scale away. Instead of relying on a number, focus on how you feel physically, mentally, and emotionally.

## Eating Food for Life

My wellness plan used to consist of limiting diets, grueling and unenjoyable exercise, and feeling as if I were missing out on the foods I loved because they were not on my meal plan. In my twenties, I ate fat-free foods (engineered food) because I didn't know better. Now I know better, so I eat better. I read labels, and if something has too many ingredients, I don't eat it. I avoid as much chemically-engineered or packaged food as possible. "No farm, no food" is my new mantra. But let's face it: a carrot stick doesn't always cut it. I just try and enjoy foods that are good for me and that I like.

There are so many delicious foods that are good for you! Try choosing whole foods and limiting processed foods and see both how simple it is and how great you feel. Sure, I occasionally enjoy a decadent dessert. But splurging for me now is not an everyday thing. I'm learning moderation. It isn't easy. If it were, we would all look like Skinnygirl,

---

*Having a healthy relationship with your body is important; the number on the scale is not!*

---

Bethenny Frankle. She works at it, too, and has embraced a healthy lifestyle after a journey of emotional eating and gaining weight. (You know the drill.) Most of the population are overweight, and those who are not usually work on maintaining their right size. A very few are blessed with the metabolism that makes weight maintenance natural and easy. Don't get frustrated, and don't go crazy; just do your best to make healthy food choices for each meal. And remember, healthy food choices don't have to be blah and bland. You can eat wonderful, nourishing foods that are both delicious and healthy. The bonus: They'll give you incredible energy.

## Drink to Your Health

Water is a girl's best friend. I know we love diamonds, but water is the fuel to keep us going! (Pun intended.) Water

# Tips for Healthy Living

- Avoid diets. The only plans that work are detox programs because they give a health benefit!
- Eat whole foods.
- Eat organic. Don't use price as an excuse; you are worth the extra cost!
- Eat three meals plus two snacks (or five small meals) each day.
- Drink at least sixty-eight ounces of water each day.
- Avoid refined sugar and wheat.
- Exercise at least five days a week.
- Shoot for at least eight hours of sleep each night.

# A Healthy Day for Me:

**Breakfast:** Fruit smoothie. I love these! I use almond milk and add high-quality vegan protein.

**Snack:** Fresh berries, almonds, or an apple.

**Lunch:** Either a smoothie or a salad with grilled chicken.

**Snack:** Nutrition bar, nuts, carrots and hummus, detox tea, sometimes corn chips with salsa (my indulgence).

**Dinner:** Usually fish, always grilled or baked, never fried, with salad and veggies on the side!

**Dessert:** My favorite, a few spoons full of coconut milk chocolate ice cream (so yummy). It's not low fat, but it's so good! I skip dessert if I am focused on cleansing and detoxing. I splurge in maintenance or on weekends.

helps to flush out your system and detoxify your body. Not only does it keep you hydrated, it also keeps your energy level up and helps you feel better. Water will actually help stave off cravings, so fill on up with some clean, pure $H_2O$. Add a lemon wedge to add some flavor and more cleansing and detoxifying benefits.

Good hydration benefits your body in every way: your brain, your skin, your energy level, the way your body processes food... everything. I know some of you really have a hard time guzzling the water. My advice is to give yourself a week to really focus on getting those sixty-eight ounces of water a day. Start early in the day by drinking a glass (or two) with your breakfast. I promise you will feel a difference!

> HIPP girls respect the environment. Recycle those water bottles, or better yet, get a reusable bottle and refill it.

If your mindset is *water is boring,* change your mindset! Think of water as fuel that helps your body run at its optimum level. Because I'm mindful of my water intake now, I notice on the days when I don't get enough. I've also noticed that the more I exercise, the more I crave water. Water does the body good. Drink up!

## GET MOVING!

Exercise is essential to wellness. While I have always loved to exercise, I also know it is easy to fall out of practice unless you make it a priority. For a time, I was so busy being busy I failed to realize what I really needed was extra focus on my wellness. Taking care of my physical self has empowered me to come alive and really thrive.

It's easier to remember to exercise if you enjoy the activity. My exercise has become my hobby because I enjoy it so much; you know, a love-hate relationship. There are times I have to motivate myself to get moving, but for the most part, I love it because I anticipate the energy it gives me. I have done everything from gym memberships, to running, to boot camp, to yoga, and tennis; I love them all! My must-have and priority is yoga, because it makes me feel good physically, mentally, and spiritually. I also enjoy running to music outside. I love the fresh air and scenery! If running is too much for you, start with a brisk walk. I walk my dog and sometimes listen to a book on my MP3 player. Listening to an encouraging message or a book that pertains to my work while walking is an efficient way for me to learn, grow, and exercise all at once.

If you are athletic or have been athletic, you need to stay active and fit; it is part of who you are. If you are a high-energy person like me, chances are you need physical activity to move your energy. Exercise is crucial to living a HIPP life. If you are not feeling it, then increase your exercise and you will see what I mean. The key to being effective, like anything in life, is consistent effort. Plan for exercise consistently in your schedule. Better yet, make it a priority in your day. Even though I love exercise, I used to have a hard time trying to fit it in. You know how that goes. Despite my good intentions, I never seemed to have enough time. Now I make exercise the first thing I do after I get my kids off to school. I'm still busy, but now there's always time for exercise because it's a priority for me. A priority is a *non-negotiable*. I schedule my work time around my health and fitness and have benefitted from increased energy and stamina. Just try it!

## Yoga

In my business, I get to coach people on success and encourage them to break through their obstacles. I get to show them how much they have inside of them and how they can bring that to the surface. What I do in my yoga practice is bring my true self to the surface. My yoga teachers guide me to shine—to break through and go to the edge. They prepare me for life off the mat, so I can face my day with grace, strength, and integrity.

Who knew yoga could be beneficial in so many ways? I had tried to like it for the past decade. At first I thought it was weird, then I thought it was boring, then I thought it was not a good enough workout. I can count on one hand how

*Yoga encompasses the mind-body connection. It prepares your body and mind for whatever comes your way in life.*

many times I got on my mat during that decade, so you can see how hard I tried—or didn't. On a friend's recommendation, I tried Power Yoga. Wow! I have found a passion and commitment to this practice, *and* I am more peaceful, more intentional, and am learning more about me. I look and feel better than I have in twenty years! So, my friends, yoga is great and I highly recommend it to everyone. Find the right yoga studio and a yoga practice you can get comfortable with. Let yourself be changed from the inside out! The name of my yoga studio is Empower, and I cannot think of a better name to describe what this practice has done for me. Yoga encompasses the mind-body connection. It prepares your body and mind for whatever comes your way in life. The strong warrior poses remind us that we are warriors, stronger and more capable than we realize. The practice of being present in the moment calls us not just to be present on the mat, but in life and in our relationships.

If you are seeking clarity, simplicity, or peace in your life, I encourage you to start a yoga practice. If you believe you don't have time, imagine I'm putting my hands on my hips and reminding you that you are stating a priority, not a fact. I understand "busy" and have used that excuse in the past. But being well is all about creating time and making choices that strengthen and nourish you. Maybe you need to say no to something else, so you can say yes to your health and to a whole new you! Stop hiding behind your business, family, or volunteer work, and start showing up for yourself.

*Namaste*, my friends!

# HIPP TIPS FOR LIVING WELL ON & OFF THE MAT

- Be open.
- Be yourself.
- Remind yourself you have everything inside of you.
- Be balanced: too much of one thing is not a good thing.
- Go with the flow.
- Be focused.
- Let your light shine.
- Nurture yourself.
- Love yourself.
- Simplify.
- Don't push: attract.
- Breathe.
- Be mindful.
- Fuel your body.
- Hydrate.
- Stand strong.
- Try.
- Stretch.
- Go to the edge.
- Get out of your comfort zone.
- Pray.
- Be present.
- See good in all things.
- Love what is.
- Practice self-care.
- Rest.

# Get HIPP!

*You were made to live
Happy, Inspired, Passionate, and Peaceful!*

**B**y now I'm sure you have given some serious thought to your HIPP life. What will it take for you to live HIPP? Are you in for small changes or does your life need a complete renovation? Whether the changes you plan to make are big or small, commitment, awareness, and mindfulness are essential. To live HIPP, you must fully believe that you were not only beautifully made; you were made to live Happy, Inspired, Passionate, and Peaceful. Today, right now, is your moment to stand up and OWN your HIPP life. It is time for you to kick some SASS! Live it, be it, do it.

We all know that it can be tough to feel HIPP day in and day out. Life is messy. That's why awareness is critical! It's okay—normal even—to get down, or too busy, or stressed, but that doesn't mean you have to stay that way! You can choose to laugh your way out of a bad mood. Or maybe what you need is another HIPP chic, someone who will pull you off the hamster wheel and into a better, HIPP life.

Sometimes, reading quotes like those listed below gives me the encouragement I need to get my groove back. The following are quotes from people whose words have had a powerful influence on my life. It is my hope that you'll use these words of wisdom when you need a dose of inspiration. Read and re-read them. Copy your favorites and post them on your bathroom mirror, right beside your HIPP Affirmations. Become aware of what you're choosing to think about and be mindful of how those thoughts energize you… or drain you. Quotes are only the beginning—they are tools to remind you to take action. Take action on your attitude; take action on your disposition; take action on achieving your goals. When you take action, you can move from point A to point B; you can reach your goals, dreams, and desires. Like my mentor Rita Davenport says, you've got to mind your mind and then you've got to move. Let this "kick-SASS" advice from the masters help you do exactly that so you can get HIPP!

# Kick-SASS Advice

## On Attitude

"A strong, positive self-image is the best possible preparation for success." —*Joyce Brothers*

"Shoot for the moon, if you miss, at least you'll land among the stars!" —*Les Brown*

"Any fool can criticize, condemn, and complain, but it takes character and self-control to be understanding and forgiving." —*Dale Carnegie*

"Nothing is more important than reconnecting with your bliss. Nothing is as rich. Nothing is more real."
—*Deepak Chopra*

"Nothing is more important than a sense of humor. I've found it's the most underrated secret of success. The physical and chemical results of laughter can create a million-dollar mind. A smile may not solve your problems, but it will mess with people who are trying to mess with you!"
—*Rita Davenport*

"If you can dream it, you can do it." —*Walt Disney*

"A man is what he thinks about all day long."
—*Ralph Waldo Emerson*

"I release all criticism. I only give out that which I wish to receive in return. My love and acceptance of others is mirrored to me in every moment." —*Louise Hay*

"Happiness is not something ready-made. It comes from your own actions." —*Dalai Lama*

"If you want more, you have to require more of yourself."
—*Phil McGraw*

"Believing you are worthy of love means that you believe I deserve to be treated well, with respect and dignity. I deserve to be cherished and adored by someone. I am worthy of an intimate and fulfilling relationship. I won't settle for less than I deserve. I will do whatever it takes to create that for myself." — *Suze Orman*

"More than anything else, I believe it's our decisions, not the conditions of our lives, that determine our destiny." —*Tony Robbins*

"Life is 10 percent of what happens to me and 90 percent of how I react to it." —*Charles Swindoll*

"Life isn't as serious as the mind makes it out to be." —*Eckhart Tolle*

## On Fear

"Imagine what you'd do if it absolutely didn't matter what people thought of you. Got it? Good. Never go back." —*Martha Beck*

"Don't let the fear of the time it will take to accomplish something stand in the way of your doing it. The time will pass anyway; we might just as well put that passing time to the best possible use." —*Earl Nightingale*

"Our deepest fear is not that we are inadequate. Our deepest fear is that we are powerful beyond measure. It is our light, not our darkness that most frightens us. We ask ourselves, 'Who am I to be brilliant, gorgeous, talented, fabulous?' Actually, who are you not to be? You are a child of God. Your playing small does not serve the world. There is nothing enlightened about shrinking so that other people won't feel insecure around you. We are all meant to shine, as children do. We were born to make manifest the glory of God that is within us. It's not just in some of us; it's in everyone. And as we let our own light shine, we unconsciously give other people permission to do the same. As we are liberated from our own fear, our presence automatically liberates others." —*Marianne Williamson*

## On Growing

"Every adversity, every failure, every heartache carries with it the seed of an equal or greater benefit."
—*Napoleon Hill*

"Take the first step in faith. You don't have to see the whole staircase. Just take the first step." —*Martin Luther King, Jr.*

"If someone is going down the wrong road, he doesn't need motivation to speed him up; he needs education to turn him around." —*Jim Rohn*

"When you're through changing, you're through."
—*Martha Stewart*

"Don't dwell on what went wrong. Instead, focus on what to do next. Spend your energies on moving forward toward finding the answer." —*Denis Waitley*

## On Making a Difference

"I've learned that people will forget what you said, people will forget what you did, but people will never forget how you made them feel." —*Maya Angelou*

"Alone we can do so little; together we can do so much."
—*Helen Keller*

"A man may die, nations may rise and fall, but an idea lives on." —*John F. Kennedy*

"You are the leader you've been looking for."
—*Marie Shriver*

## On Achieving

"The more clearly someone sees the future, the more confidently they work in the present." —*Dr. Tom Barrett*

"The problem is that most people focus on their failures rather than their successes. But the truth is that most people have many more successes than failures."
—*Jack Canfield*

"An MBA doesn't impress me. A GSD does. GSD = Gets Stuff Done." —*Christine Comaford*

"For me, the most important thing in your life is to live your life with integrity and not to give in to peer pressure, to try to be something that you're not. To live your life as an honest and compassionate person. To contribute in some way." —*Ellen DeGeneres*

"Dreaming is fun, but doing is much more rewarding." —*Tory Johnson*

"The only place success comes before work is in the dictionary." —*Vince Lombardi*

"Always seek out the seed of triumph in every adversity." —*Og Mandino*

"Do something you really love that you would do anyway; do it in the most adventurous place, and if there's a genuine need for it and through that need you can help other people, you're home." —*Diane Sawyer*

"All successful people men and women are big dreamers. They imagine what their future could be, ideal in every respect, and then they work every day toward their distant vision, that goal or purpose." —*Brian Tracy*

"Writing is the gold standard of communication. Learn to do it well and see more gold." —*Chris Widener*

"Surround yourself with only people who are going to lift you higher." —*Oprah Winfrey*

"Money isn't the most important thing in life, but it's reasonably close to oxygen on the 'gotta have it' scale." —*Zig Ziglar*

# Passing It On

I've told you that Rita Davenport has been a mentor and a huge influence in my life. She is a master encourager! Rita is known for sharing funny insights and for studying and passing on lessons she's learned from others. Below are a few of the many things I've learned from her. She'll tell you she picked up some of these quotes from other encouragers. Some she's learned through her own hard-earned experience. Regardless of their original source, I'm thankful to Rita for using her voice to inspire me and countless others. *Enjoy!*

"Success requires three bones: a wishbone, a backbone, and a funnybone!"

"What you think about you bring about."

"Your greatest gift is loving and believing in yourself. Guard this gift always. It's a breakthrough to being able to love and believe in others."

"People perceive your love and belief; it grows everyone's confidence."

"Be nicer than necessary."

"Fake it 'til you make it!"

"Get rid of your stinkin' thinkin'. Give yourself a mental enema."

"You need at least three hugs a day to be 'normal.'"

"The secret to happiness is good health and a short memory!"

"Forgive yourself first. Then it's easier to forgive others."

"Anger is like drinking poison and expecting the other person to die."

"Never turn your power or well-being over to someone else."

"You only have eighteen summers with your children."

"If you keep doing what you're doing, you're going to keep getting what you're getting."

"Help enough people get what they want and you'll always get what you want."

"If you're looking for a helping hand, look at the end of your sleeve!"

"If you have a problem and money can fix it... then it ain't really a problem."

"Nothing is more attractive than a rich woman."

"Your net worth in this life has to do with your network."

"The world steps aside for the woman who knows where she's going."

"Give up what you love for a little while, so you can do what you want to do forever."

"Change is the only constant in life. Except for a baby with wet diapers, most of us resist change. Instead, train yourself to use change as an endless source of inspiration, motivation, creativity, and productivity."

"Mama told me, 'Don't get such high hopes.'" But I asked myself, 'Well, what durn good are low hopes?'"

"There's nothing but you holding you back."

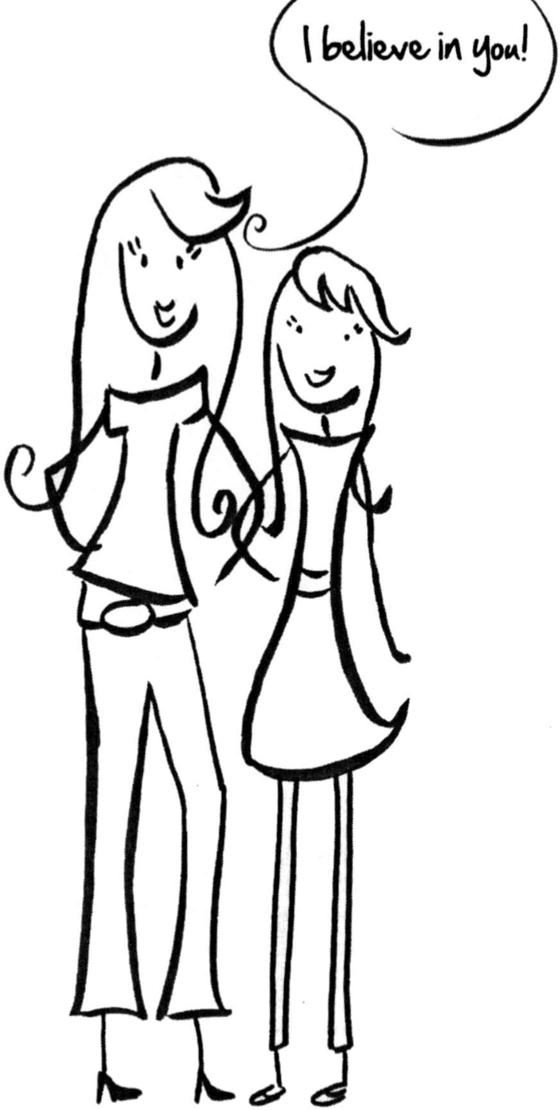
I believe in you!

# HIPP GENERATION

**We are all connected
at the HIPP!**

Living HIPP feels good. It feels fantastic! So why not share the love? Remember, we all influence each other either positively or negatively... we are all connected at the HIPP! So, decide today to positively influence people with your HIPPness! Living HIPP isn't all about you. It's about how you show up and make a difference in the world. Sure, you start with you. You heal and help yourself first. But somewhere along your journey, you'll discover that the only way you can really live HIPP is by helping and influencing others through your example to do the same. Living HIPP is more than a book or a brand; it is a culture, a way to live. It is my hope that Living HIPP will become a sisterhood that empowers women, teens, and girls to live their best, most authentic lives.

Welcome to the HIPP Generation, a team of women, and a few HIPP men, who live our own HIPP lives and encourage each other to dare to live our dreams. This team shares a bond. The synergy that occurs when we unite with commitment and teamwork to bring out HIPP in others is nothing short of amazing.

We are in this together, my HIPP friend. As part of the HIPP Generation, I hope you will commit to:

- Treating others the way you want to be treated.

- Opening your heart and sharing your struggles, successes, and humor with others.

- Focusing on solutions, not problems.

- Standing strong, with hands on hips, to support, teach and inspire girls and teens to create their HIPP lives.

- Creating a positive environment for yourself and others.

- Seeing and praising HIPP in others.

- Confronting mean-girls and bullies.

- Laughing at yourself, often!

- Remembering not to take life too seriously!

- Using your voice to encourage, inspire, and uplift others.

- Changing what needs to be changed. Don't wait for someone else to act.

- Blazing a path for others to follow.

- Helping teens and younger women live their best, HIPP life.

Let's work together to create a HIPP sensation of women, teens, and girls recognizing and rewarding HIPP in others. Grab the "Tag You're HIPP" button from LivingHIPP.com, and tag the HIPP people in your life. Let them know you see and appreciate their kindness, love, generosity, authenticity, courage, tenacity, strength, humor, patience—any of the qualities that really matter in life. The button is free, and tagging someone is fun; it feels good! Seeing and encouraging the best in others brings out the best in you!

# How Can You Help?

Share the HIPPness! Tell everyone you know about *Living HIPP*. The more people embrace HIPP, the more powerful our gender is. This is not about "women's lib." Women are already incredibly powerful. When we join forces and empower each other, I believe we can change the world for the better—beyond anything we have ever done. And it starts with you. Kick some sass in your own life by Living HIPP and by sharing the concept of Living HIPP—the book and the philosophy it embodies—with everyone you know. Get on Facebook and Twitter and share!

Here is my button to you, Thank you for being part of our HIPP Generation!

# I Am Committed To Living HIPP!

My new HIPP daily attitude is:

_____

_____

_____

_____

_____

_____

_____

_____

My "Hands-on-Hip" statement on fear is:

_____

_____

_____

_____

_____

_____

_____

_____

My daily commitment to growth is:

_____

_____

_____

_____

_____

The HIPP difference I want to make in the world is:

_____

_____

_____

_____

_____

_____

My HIPP dream is:

_____

_____

_____

_____

_____

I will remove the following people, things, habits, or attitudes in order to reach my dreams:

_____

_____

_____

_____

_____

_____

_____

The goal I will achieve this year is (be specific and set a date):

_____

_____

_____

_____

_____

_____

_____

_____

_____

My HIPP Life Mission Statement is:

_____

_____

_____

_____

_____

_____

_____

_____

_____

_____

I hope you've enjoyed this HIPP journey. Now it's time to share *Living HIPP* with the women in your life! Join the HIPP Generation by living HIPP and bringing out the HIPP in others. Mahatma Gandhi said, "Be the change you want to see in the world." I'm going to ask you to go a step further: *Share* the HIPP you want to see in the world.

~~~

Do you know a teen who would benefit from the message of HIPP? Watch for my upcoming book, *HIPP Teens.* Read on the next page about how you can make a difference in a young woman's life through the HIPP HOP mission!

# HIPP ADVICE FOR THE NEXT GENERATION

- Always believe in yourself.
- Trust your gut. If something doesn't feel good, or right, it isn't.
- Protect your body from boys, drugs, alcohol, etc. Your body is sacred.
- Protect your mind. Always be clear and in control.
- Say no—to boys, friends, adults, or situations that are inappropriate. Saying no will help you avoid doing something you'll regret later.
- Follow your dreams. You can do anything!
- Study and work hard. Don't worry about being the best; just do your personal best.
- Don't compare yourself to anyone. You are unique—own that!
- Be sassy. Stand up for yourself with your hands on your hips!
- Be classy. Don't put others down.
- Listen to, share with, support, and love your friends.
- Be friends with only those who are nice to you at all times. Make sure your friends are worthy of you.
- Raise the bar. Expect yourself to succeed.
- Be compassionate with yourself and others.
- Know you are loved by God and your family.
- Remember, there is always someone to help you.

# HIPP HOP
## HIPP PeopLe HeLpiNG OTHeR PeopLe

You have already made a difference in someone's life. Not simply by being an amazing and inspiring person, but by purchasing this book, you are supporting the HIPP HOP mission. One dollar from every copy of *Living HIPP* sold will be used to fund this nonprofit mission focused on helping women and teens live HIPP. **My goal is to raise $1 million to help increase awareness about and stop bullying and abuse.**

I hope you'll help us spread the word and create a world of HIPP. Your HIPPness is a gift. Why not share that gift with everyone by becoming a HIPP Ambassador? It costs nothing, but the world has everything to gain from your example.

If you have ever been treated unfairly by that thoughtless girl in middle school, grade school, or high school, help us raise awareness about this problem by promoting a HIPP lifestyle and by sharing *Living HIPP* with everyone you know. If you have been abused, or know someone who has been abused, choose to be an empowering example of HIPP.

Abuse and bullying are wrong and need to stop! I am committed to the HIPP HOP mission of ending bullying and child abuse. Will you join me? When you share *Living HIPP* and the HIPP brand, you are helping to change this world, one HIPP person at a time.

***Live HIPP!***

# ACKNOWLEDGEMENTS

Since this is my first book, I feel the need to offer a long "I'd like to thank the academy" speech. Seriously, the people in my life who inspire me have helped me become who I am today. Those who are listed here (and many who are not) have not only left their fingerprint on me, they helped make this book possible. Thank you.

In terms of making this book a reality, there are a few HIPP people I would like to thank. First of all, I want to thank Tory Johnson, because she helped me move from talking about Living HIPP and treating it like a hobby, to turning it into a brand, a book, and a goal. Tory, you are the small-business guru. Your ability to make things happen, is remarkable. You were the coach who believed in me and drafted me onto the team. You not only showed me the playbook, you ran through the plays with me several times. Thank you.

My other coach is my book coach and editor extraordinaire, Erin Casey. Erin, you embraced this project with such excitement about HIPP and all the possibilities. We went from all my ideas, stories, initiatives, and pages of writing, to a well-written, practical, and relatable book I believe will inspire millions. Thank you for your excellent work. You took my words and emotions and captured a final message that engages the reader and leaves them wanting more.

Another big thank you goes to my friend Amanda Edwards. Amanda, you read all of my drafts during the months I spent second-guessing myself and wanting to quit. You hung with me—loving on me, correcting me, and encouraging me to provide more from my heart. You held the bar high and supported me when I felt vulnerable from "writers remorse."

*Living HIPP* wouldn't be nearly so hip without the contribution of illustrator Erin Clark. Erin, thank you for giving the HIPP brand a beautiful face. You are an amazingly talented artist!

While the book was being written, the brand came together with the help of my assistant Maggie Ruch. Thank you, Maggie for your talent and work on the website and Facebook page, and for creating the infrastructure to support the book and the mission to help every girl, teen, and woman live HIPP.

While I worked and let the laundry, dishes, and dirt pile up, my girl Nicole was there to make my house the home I love and the home my family deserves. Thank you, Nicole!

Thank you to my ghost readers, Kathy, Amanda, Joanne, Donna, Cecilia, Carla, Amy, I loved hearing from you and seeing this resonate; your excitement on "not being able to put it down" built me up. I chose you because I see the HIPP in you!

I want to also thank the incredible thought leaders, icons, and game changers who embraced the HIPP mission and gladly wrote endorsements. I admire each one of these professionals, and it is an honor and privilege to have you as a top ambassador of HIPP: Sallie Felton, Darren Hardy, Donna Johnson, Tory Johnson, Allyson Lewis, Dan Miller, and Chris Widener.

Thank you to my mentors: First and foremost, Rita Davenport (whom many of us refer to as our white Oprah). You changed my life. You set an example of someone I wanted to be like. You believed in me and assured me I could do anything I wanted to do. The way you speak to an audience is something I have never seen anywhere else. I believe you could write the book on how to create culture, because that is exactly what you did in our business. I look forward to telling everyone about your upcoming book. (It's a guaranteed home run!) Thank you for teaching me how to put on my big-girl pants, how to hug myself and love myself, how to laugh at myself, how to love others, and how to go after my dreams. I love you, and I love being your "baby girl!"

Oprah Winfrey, you don't know me, but I believe that's going to change someday soon. (I've got my mind set and my hands on hips about that!) You have been a constant source of inspiration to me. Even though you speak to millions, you speak to me. You are an extraordinary example of courage, hope, wisdom, faith, dreams, and reinvention. During the past twenty-five years you have made me laugh, you have inspired me, you have educated me, and you have touched my heart. More recently, the teachings in your *Master Class* on following your purpose and listening to God's whisper, has really touched me. This book and my next chapter are an example of me listening to you and trusting what I don't see, but rather, what I feel. I am excited about OWN and about how it helps HIPP girls strive to live their best life. I believe people should watch OWN so they can OWN their lives!

I want to thank all of my business partners in my company. You have taught me so much, and supported me in every way. My business has taught me so much about Living HIPP, and it is the people in the business that truly make it meaningful and so much fun. Thank you: Joanne, Michelle, Caitlin, Phoebe, Robin, Phyllis, Denise, Shan, Stacey, Dana, Kathy, and all of the HIPP people on our team! All of the sideline friends and VP's, you inspire me more than you know. A special thanks also to Kay and Gina for the positive support and encouragement. I also want to acknowledge people who were part of my business at one time. You are always a member of my team, and are HIPP in every way. My life is better because of all of you.

I want to acknowledge my yoga instructors and studio. My yoga practice helped me move through this process. The HIPP brand was brainstormed when I did a consistent practice at the studio; I used the poses to prepare my body and soul to give birth to something that is bigger than I. I know without my practice, I would not have been able to "warrior" through with ideas, obstacles, and connections like I have. I love you, Empower Yoga Studio: Tricia, Elizabeth and all of the instructors. A shout out to all of my yogi friends, *Namaste*!

There are too many to mention, but I want to thank all of these people from these phases in my life:
- RHS friends, teachers, and neighbors (Kathy and Chris) ... (I'm a proud "Rockland Chick!")
- College friends and Professors (my HIPP gal pals Sue, Julie and Kellie)
- Deaconess: Thank you to friend and mentor Alesia Latson

- BI Hospital (special thanks to Kim Johnson, my twenty-something gal pal)
- CTP Colleagues and friends
- Georgetown neighbors/Beverly Friends (Love you, Martha Palmer!)
- H/W moms and friends: I am so proud of you (so many to list, but you ALL inspire me). Thank you!
- Dance moms (a shout-out to my duo partner, Steph), let's bring Abby Lee some HIPP, rather than lip!
- Hockey moms (Krista, you are so HIPP!)
- Spark & Hustle (MM) BBF's
- HIPP girls that lived with me and helped me with my babies: Shano, Adelle, Alta, and Melissa. I love you girls and can't wait to see you continue to grow HIPP!
- Jenn O, you are a beautiful soul; thanks for being on my HIPP journey with me.

Being a highly spirited, feisty girl also comes with conflict and challenge. I want to acknowledge those who have challenged me. While I am not always grateful for that, I am grateful for the experience of learning to live with integrity, grace, and forgiveness. Many experiences where I have not been appreciated, loved, or respected, have given me opportunity to grow, make mistakes, make great choices, learn, and eventually thrive as the strong woman I am today. These challenges have been turned into opportunities to rise above and transform hurt into heart, which is incredibly healing. I wish the same for you.

Of course, special, heartfelt thanks to my entire family, extended and all.

Growing up Mellor, I am so proud of my family. Mom, you are sweet, kind, and loving. You always believed in me and made me feel special. You made our home and family life HIPP! You and Dad instilled in me the importance of family; I love you so much, Mom. Dad, you would be so proud. My life is beautiful and your spirit shines inside me. You were right: We were not rich but we were wealthy in love and family. I admire you even more today because you took your obstacles and created opportunity, a loving family, and a home. You were so incredibly strong, and I am going to stand up and fight now that you can't.

To my brothers and sisters: You shaped who I am, making me fight for my position (hands on hips), and giving me love and protection. I love wearing *Mellor* on the back of my shirt.

Peg and Bob, my in-laws, I love you like parents. You have been so good to me. Margaret, I love you, girlfriend. I will forever cherish our days of babies and friendship; thank you. Bumpa, you are the nicest man I know, for real! The entire Guyer family not only took me in, but dubbed me the "Jacqueline Kennedy" in our family. Wow, talk about rags to riches. I love you all! To all my nieces and nephews: Brianna, Rorrie, Bryce, Christian, McKenzie, Kayla, Shelby, Kelsey, Shae, Maya—know how special you are and how much Auntie loves you—always live HIPP.

To my husband Charlie: We are a team. We put our family first, and we equally contribute and make our busy life somehow not only work, but thrive! I could never do it without you. You are the most amazing father and husband. No one makes me laugh more than you; I love you. We are like peas and carrots! HIPP family all the way!

Kaili, I want to be more like you. You are funny, loving, caring, and the best friend ever. We are so proud of you. You are the poster girl for Living HIPP!

Cameron, your strength and determination are gifts, your humor and talent are fun, and we are so proud of you. We adore you.

Colby, you are gifted in many ways: funny, smart, and sweet. You love your family more than anything, and we love that about you.

I want to thank God for all of my blessings. The best way any of us can thank Him is by living our HIPP life, and being a shining example of encouraging HIPP in the world. HIPP is the opposite of bullying. Love is the best gift you can share. Stand up for yourself, and stand up for each other. I want to acknowledge anyone that has been bullied in any way in their life. It could have been physical, emotional, or sexual, peer to peer, or adult to child. It is wrong; it is not going to be tolerated. Embrace HIPP, live HIPP, teach HIPP. Get behind the HIPP HOP mission to acknowledge this important cause with me.

Finally, I thank you, my HIPP girlfriend! My readers, the women, teens, and girls who are part of this HIPP Generation. Inside every girl is a beautiful example of HIPP and a desire to shine brightly in this world. This is your opportunity to stand out, stand up, and stand together to make a difference, not only in your life, but in others' lives, as well. HIPP is a difference-maker; it is a reminder to live your best life, to give your best to others, and to see the best in them. Tag, you're HIPP!

# About the Author

**Pam Guyer** is the queen of Living HIPP! As a wife, mother, author, speaker, direct sales leader, and brand ambassador, Guyer is passionate about living life on her own terms. With more than twenty years' experience in leadership and business development, as well as in teaching work/life balance, Guyer combines her expertise with her vision of a HIPP world to empower women and teens to own their lives.

In addition to earning a master's degree in training and development, Guyer is a successful entrepreneur and has coached countless women on achieving success in business and life. She believes every girl deserves to live HIPP!

Guyer lives on the north shore of Boston with her husband Charlie, their three children, and dog Brady.

CPSIA information can be obtained at www.ICGtesting.com
Printed in the USA
BVOW010834050412

286929BV00005B/1/P